The Deanna Durbin *Fairy Tale*

W. E. Mills

Ro

First published in Great Britain 1996 by
Riverstone Ltd
Ireland.

British Library Cataloguing in Publication Data

A catalogue record for this book is available
from the British Library

ISBN 0 9521265 3 2

Designed by Anita Sherwood
Cover design by Chris Redman
Produced by Images Publishing (Malvern) Ltd.
Printed in Great Britain by BPC Wheatons Ltd, Exeter

Contents

F o r e w o r d

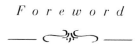

Born in Canada, of English parents Deanna Durbin began her film career at the age of fourteen in a Metro-Goldwyn Meyer film, called 'Every Sunday'. A little cameo role of twenty minutes' duration, she sang role with Judy Garland, then a young girl like herself. She made her first full-length film with Universal Studios, the memorable 'Three Smart Girls'. This came to the screen in 1936 and was the prelude to a remarkable and successful series of films, most of which had a fairy-like structure. All told she starred in twenty-one major films during the years 1936-48 until her retirement from Universal Studios for whom she worked exclusively throughout her Hollywood career. Under the guidance of directors and producers of great skill she became a top box-office personality.

In this survey my aim has been to give some idea of the nature of the Universal films in question as much as words may contrive to enhance their imagery and revive a magic spell of long ago. To my mind they encapsulate many of the human qualities which have been my main preoccupation in the appraisal which follows, the true spirit of joy and emanations of love and laughter and compassionate goodwill.

As for the material set forth in the script, it is not in any sense biographical in respect of any actor or actress involved in the films, least of all Deanna Durbin herself. My text in this review is strictly what it was designed to be – a celebration of a series of Universal's films.

Collectively the films have connotations of a fairy-tale of many parts and they are rich in the spiritual images which floated bewitchingly across our screens in the Golden Age of Cinema, albeit interpretation was mainly monochrome.

I chose the title because of the ethereal and mysterious quality inseparable from the personality of the star herself and many of the films made during her brief career when she was a veritable princess of Hollywood. Those of us who are of the same generation remember those days with joy and nostalgia, if not with veneration. Despite the films being made in the bleak texture of black and white (save the delightful 'Can't Help Singing') they were hewn of wonderment. Nor shall our memory ever dim of her wonderful singing voice, so youthful, so tender and tuneful, which entranced millions with a succession of delightful arias and melodies performed with an artistry which has never been excelled in the history of the cinema. Close to our hearts do we clutch that memory like a talisman never to be relinquished. There was little electronic gadgetry in the Thirties and Forties when we listened enthralled to the sound of her inimitable voice, but so natural was her performance, so consummate, that no technology was required to enhance it. In a world where the beat of pop music persistently assails the ear the strains of Deanna's sweet voice singing Tosti's 'Goodbye' are balm to the tortured spirit.

C h a p t e r   1

An Introduction to Deanna

I t might be trite to pose the question – what was the secret of Deanna's instant appeal when she first appeared before the cameras? The secret, if so it can be called, is to my mind simply her capacity for uplifting the human soul, to banish gloom from the oppressed spirit.

Writers have told of her 'dancing eyes' – Franchot Tone called her 'Shy Eyes' (after the tragic Indian in 'Nice Girl'?) – but she soon left the 'childish eyes' of 'Three Smart Girls' behind her as the years passed. With their passage came what I can only describe as a period of transfiguration. Her eyes certainly danced with the joy of life, growing ever more lustrous. Their soulfulness on occasions nowise dimmed their brilliance. Through that lattice penetrated the soft glow of a warm and loveable personality. Not ever did a hint of mischief in their depths extinguish her youthful innocence, an innocence which in her films was often a shield against what must have seemed brutal realities, and a salve for the dilemmas which were constantly recurring.

'Fairy princess', a description often employed by critics in the Thirties to convey the breathtaking nature of her appearance in the film world, is by no means an exaggeration. The harsh decade of the Thirties was in dire need of a new religion to help disperse the overpowering gloom and pessimism which had insinuated itself into all walks of life. In the world of entertainment Deanna, often spirited, ever unaffected, the epitome of feminine charm, did much to provide a stimulus to the required faith. The pure and touching spontaneity with which she broke into song in most of her films was an absolute dream of delight. There was nothing cerebral about Deanna's inspiration – it was rooted in her heart and permeated her whole being. Let me pause here in this preamble to make a modest allusion to the impressions and reactions she evoked in me, and similar feelings it well may be in so many other admirers scattered across this Earth. Most of us are ageing. Can you blame us for clinging with tenacity to a dream we hold most dear?

My first observation must be that I count myself lucky to have been born just a few years before Deanna Durbin and to have lived through the same century. To me this lovely lady was not a comet flashing brightly in the skies, but a nova which lights up a whole galaxy. The songs she sang in her brief but brilliant film career are to me a diapason which seems more emblematic of what we humans call 'heaven', and by heaven (no expletive here) I mean something that accords with my idea of perfection and withal so mysterious that it cannot be truly analysed.

I was about twenty-one when I first saw the film 'Three Smart Girls' and like thousands of other young men of my generation I was captivated by Deanna's innocent charm and loveliness. Even the anger and petulance her part called for at times did not detract from the exquisite sweetness which was intrinsically hers. As she matured I became more and more infatuated with this glorious creature who sang so beautifully and played her film roles with a superb conviction. How tense I was in her later films when she was caught in a difficult situation – remember how she closed her eyes in an agony of suspense in the final scenes of 'The Amazing Mrs Holliday' when the commodore mounted the dais, having expressed his intention of addressing a crowded hall? I thought to myself – 'what a monster if he exposes her to humiliation in public!' Fictitious though the circumstances were, there was a poignancy in that scene which might have moved the least impressionable of viewers. And what of Deanna's face breaking into that familiar radiant smile when the commodore seemed to have second thoughts, saying nothing about a spurious marriage? Reflecting on that incident my mind goes back to Deanna's early days in films, to 'Mad About Music' and her agitation and acute embarrassment when her 'adopted' father, played by Herbert Marshall, addressed her class in a Swiss high school. He certainly gave the impression that he was about to expose a fraud, but Deanna's expression, eyes tightly closed in suspense and trepidation, her whole attitude one of suppressed misery, melted his heart. What a technique she had for emphasising the pathos of a situation! Your one desire was to hold her in a protective embrace, if not to send packing in summary fashion those responsible for any emotional pain inflicted upon her. There were times too involving the willing sacrifice of her own ambitions and happiness to serve the interests of others when her voice softened perceptibly, those glorious eyes misted and her lips quivered. Her air was that of a rejected angel. All the nuances of self-sacrifice came so naturally in expression and gesture in her portrayal of characters tormented by frustration or misfortune. In a converse way her smiles and laughter were irresistible. Oh, it is so easy to slip into a panegyric when speaking of a uniquely lovely, talented girl and woman, one moreover with a voice (not 'one in a million' as the trite phrase runs) but one that is as rare on Earth as a sunburst in the heavens. I may not be educated in a professional or vocational way to judge the intrinsic quality of a voice, its resonance and musical timbre, etcetera. What I am sure of is that the voice of Deanna Durbin, as it is heard on film or record, is the most thrilling, the most soothing and mellifluous I have ever heard in this world, or may hope to in the next (for if I am no true believer in immortality I am no atheist either). Deanna was at her best singing the lovely ballads and melodies of yesterday and arias which ring out like a peal of bells to enliven opera

– for opera, alas, can be so often tedious and heavy in composition. It can be more cerebral than artistic in interpretation. In respect of what I would term the songs of a more gracious and leisurely age than our own – videlicet, the age of the bustle, the early phonograph, the horse-drawn carriage – I have been surprised how seldom the film and television media of today broadcast the kind of traditional songs in which Deanna excelled in her splendid repertoire. What heart could fail to be moved when she sang 'The Last Rose of Summer' before daddy Winniger delivered false and unkind judgement on the quality of her voice in 'Three Smart Girls Grow Up'. Her rendering of 'Home Sweet Home' in 'First Love' and 'Going Home' in 'It Started with Eve', full of that inexpressible sadness and yearning which rends the sensitive heart, is more symphonic to my mind than operatic fulminations.

Deanna's high notes did not jar the nerves as do those of some sopranos who belt out their lyrics with more passion than euphony, conjuring fears of a tonsular explosion. But they do send exquisite shivers down the spine, as Connie's friend put it after the graduation ceremony in 'First Love'. I suspect that, unlike Deanna, whose voice rang out with effortless ease and magical intonation as if she herself revelled in the pleasure it gave others, music took secondary place to their egos. How restrained and wistful was Deanna's singing of 'An Old Refrain', a tune of bygone days, to her family of eight children in 'The Amazing Mrs Holliday'. There she sat in a flowing gown and antique bonnet – she whose mother 'taught her how to sing' – a picture of perfect innocence, so guileless, so adorable, so full of beauty and grace and, of all images of life one might wish to preserve in perpetuity, the ineradicable archetype.

There are songs and melodies in Deanna's films which in this tuneless and clamorous age of pop I have never heard over the radio waves. For instance, 'Tosti's Goodbye' in 'Because of Him'. Such glorious singing there was in an elevator and through the hall and corridors of a hotel to the swing doors of the vestibule whence a thoroughly egotistical and insensitive playwright escapes into the street (and into limbo, for all I care as I watch that film). I and no doubt millions of Deanna's votaries would have stood transfixed with joy just to have been the recipients of a cascade of beautiful sound; haunting, mellifluous notes; pure, lilting harmony not to be excelled, nor, I'll wager, ever bewitched human ear in the past. And there are so many other melodies which benighted television producers seem to ignore, for instance, 'My Heart is Singing' from 'Three Smart Girls', not forgetting 'Someone to Care for Me' from the same film.

Even if there were a gifted voice today to revive those melodies I doubt whether it might do so with the utter sincerity of a young Deanna and with such complete lack of sophistication. The list of songs is endless. 'It's Raining Sunbeams' from '100 Men and a Girl' is never heard to day to inspire the fairy-tale images which Deanna evoked, so long ago it seems. And 'Chapel Bells', which was doubtless sung in drawing-rooms to a rapt circle of family and friends long before the era of jazz and jive, has presumably been discarded like 'Serenade to the Stars' as being too sentimental and naive for modern audiences. Perhaps Deanna's wonderful musical interpretations do not accord with the ideas of what to modern broadcasters is fashionable, though I do not doubt that there are multitudes of older folk like me who would refute the assumption that beautiful songs can become moribund in a so-called more progressive age. These are the obsessions of a world hypnotised by trivia of all kinds, its pretentious, popular music like a chiaroscuro of sound from which all sweetness has been eliminated – ghastly syncopation and repetitive rhythms – jungle beat and mumbo-jumbo for the poetic word.

I can think of exceptions to the prevalent taste, however, like that perennial Scottish hymn, 'Loch Lomond'; but whoever sang it with the ineffable appeal and captivating warmth of Deanna's version in 'It's a Date'? And what of 'Amapola' which our inspired songstress sang with gusto in 'First Love'? Forgotten? But how it brightened the bleak days of wartime England as people flocked to the cinemas to hear Deanna Durbin sing. That dreamy extravaganza 'Spring Parade' brought further manna as it were to a famished world – the source on this occasion being a provincial Austrian lass striding from her mountain village with an obstreperous goat. And as she made her way towards the adjacent valley she sang 'It's Foolish but it's Fun'. How delightfully ingenuous, but redolent of a timeless, fairy-tale land where there was no change to corrupt or despoil, where a centuries-old way of life of simple rusticity remained undisturbed and the purest romanticism was the song of the flowering earth. What man could fail to be enthralled by 'When April Sings', a veritable feast of lyricism, or who, having heard 'Waltzing in the Clouds', would not have felt that had indeed been his experience, and envied with his whole being the lucky composer who kissed Deanna behind a pillar? And that sentiment makes me reflect – I wonder how many of those fortunate actors of the Thirties and Forties to whom fell the pleasure of kissing Deanna ever realised how many of her anonymous male admirers would willingly have given a year of their lives for such a privilege? How many men are there like myself, votaries of 'Deanna of the Golden Voice' – and that is not intended to be a figurative title – who have not craved simply to lightly brush her hand or sense the magic of her person if perchance she happened to pass them by?

Chapter 2

Three Smart Girls

Having watched repeatedly all the major films Deanna Durbin made during her Hollywood career I found myself tempted to consider them in detail, even pen my thoughts in an objective way perhaps. I strove to avoid the platitudes which so often demean serious criticism, at the same time curbing the exuberance of one who found in those films more reason for exaltation than a source of simple pleasure. Humbly I offer those reflections.

That delightful little cameo 'Every Sunday' in which Deanna sang Arditi's 'Il Bacio' and together with Judy Garland the song 'Americana' revealed an incredible talent in a young girl. Just a bandstand concert in a public park, but how her singing brought people flocking excitedly to a previously almost deserted enclosure. Yet it was but a foretaste of the musical delights which in the following years both ravished the ear and held the spirit in the sweetest thrall. How many of both sexes would deny that they lost their hearts to that lovely girl from the moment they heard her and saw her for the very first time?

If 'Every Sunday' represented Deanna's debut in the world of the cinema it was but purely fragmentary beside her first full-length film

'Three Smart Girls'. The imagery inspired by the opening scene of this film was so intense as to make one believe it could not be sustained throughout the story. A beautiful girl is singing in a tiny, sailing craft, seemingly floating across a Swiss lake against a background of forest and mountain. There are birds in the sky, limpid waters rippling. The girl's two sisters eye the singer with tender glance and unconcealed admiration. Then their governess in a splendid chalet bordering the lake winds a horn from an upper window of the house. The sound drifts across the waters to the three occupants of the boat, whereat Deanna, in the guise of Penny Craig, the most junior member of her family – promptly dives overboard to swim ashore. She is supple as a fish as she makes for the landing stage. Her less impetuous sisters bring in their craft to a jetty and race towards the house. Penny has already reached home, dried herself and donned formal dress. But she is somewhat distraught when her sister, Kay, throws a sizeable crab-apple at the eldest sister, Joan (let it be said with more frustration than venom), who has raced on ahead of her after she has fallen headlong on the path leading to the chalet. An apple, poorly aimed, had missed Joan and whizzed through an open French window. Both Kay and Joan on entry become aware of the reason for Penny's dismay. The apple has neatly punctured a hole in the left eye of a large portrait of their father, Judson Craig, who has long since left home to live in the United States.

What a contrast that comical situation provided with the idyllic vision of the opening sequence. On the one hand a beautiful and talented young girl sings delightfully amid a glorious vista of tree-hung slopes and sprawling hills – and then the sudden transition to a cluttered drawing-room with three very troubled sisters at their wits end to conceal or otherwise patch up a painting of their father with one eye quite dismembered. Two scenes, one dreamy and evocative, the second following close upon the first and mirth-provoking, become memorable for their juxtaposition if not their affinity. Where other material in the film might be readily forgotten, such as the bluster of the business fraternity in a New York boardroom, the opening sequences of the film have a lingering fascination.

14

Incidentally, Penny is off the screen for lengthy periods but in all the scenes in which she does appear I can find no fault whatever with her performance. Fourteen or thereabouts is her age in this theatrical romp and already she is more than a competent actress, to say nothing of the outpourings of her marvellous voice. So rarely is the human ear bewitched in such a way. A peerless instrument is the description which springs to mind. And if that sounds like an encomium I make no apology.

Deanna Durbin, Barbara Road and Nan Grey in 'Three Smart Girls'.
(Reproduced courtesy of Aquarius Library)

The story of 'Three Smart Girls' is about a mother and her three daughters, two in late adolescence, the third still of school age, who live in Switzerland together with a matronly governess to supervise the girls. The father who has long abandoned his family, ten years is mentioned, to take up a business career, is living in New York. His success has made him a very rich man, in fact a millionaire. Penny's mother is plainly distressed when she reads a press headline telling of an attachment between the absent father and a glamorous American socialite. For she has always secretly nourished the hope of a reconciliation with her erstwhile spouse. Penny it is who comes up with the idea that she and her two sisters should go forthwith to New York to thwart the schemes of one whom they consider is attracted more by their father's wealth than his personal attributes, for she is young and attractive in a seductive way while he is well past his fiftieth year and perceptibly greying. The scheme is necessarily put to the governess since there is the question of the fare for three to the U.S.A. quite apart from incidental expenditure. At first, appalled by the audacious plan, or pretending to be, the governess tells them not to be foolish, but she swiftly changes her mind and decides to chaperone them overseas. Hilarious scenes follow the arrival of the little party in New York where it presents itself at the Craig mansion only to be told that the master of the house is meeting his new love for lunch at a fashionable hotel. With the ebullient Penny more resolute than ever to be the means of dissolving her father's affair with a gold-digger named Donna, who is aided and abetted by an equally rapacious mother in her designs on Judson, all advance to the designated rendezvous for luncheon. Judson is already seated at table with Donna billing and cooing beside him. Judson has had prior warning that his three daughters have arrived from Switzerland and thinks it expedient to mention the fact to Donna. He produces a photograph of his attractive brood in which Penny is about five years old and her sisters not looking much senior. He explains lamely that the children have grown up somewhat since the photograph was taken to spare his prospective bride too much of a shock. Imagine then Donna's consternation, to say nothing of Judson's, when Penny, in advance of her two sisters, yells

'Daddy!' with all her might, and whilst heads turn towards her from all directions, races jubilantly into his arms. One almost feels sorry for Donna at such an introduction to her ageing suitor's family, though as contact with the Craigs necessarily becomes more involved, she is unperturbed by the obvious dislike the three daughters conceive for her. That restaurant scene is perhaps the most mirth-provoking in the whole film. It is sheer, unadulterated fun. As the story develops we are witness to a sustained effort by the Craig girls to drive a wedge between their father and the female predators – Donna and her mother – seeking to ensnare him. They are helped in the enterprise by Judson's chief trouble-shooter who falls in love with Joan, and a wealthy member of the British aristocracy given the grand name of Viscount Michael Stuart who meets Kay and is instantly attracted to her. But alas, the collective plan fails by mischance and it is left to Penny to redeem that failure; and this she does in the first place by running away from home and having the New York police force search for her. Her father who loves her perhaps more than any other is in such a fever of anxiety that he scornfully rejects the protests of Donna and her mother whose only concern is for Judson to hold to his promise of marriage. His attitude turns to revulsion when they blame Penny for her interference with their plans. There is a most joyful reunion when the police arrive at Judson's home with Penny in tow and contemporaneously a tearful Kay falls into the arms of Michael Stuart whom she believed had left the country with Donna and her mother, bound for Europe. In fact, only the scheming socialites had boarded a transatlantic liner, outwitted by a very suave but dissembling British aristocrat. The last sequence of the film is at the quayside as a liner from Europe docks with the mother of the three girls waving from an upper deck, and our final glimpse is of the radiant face of Penny gazing in turn at her mother and father with a heart both rejoicing and overflowing with tenderness.

In this first major film role Deanna sings three beautiful songs, 'My heart is Singing' in the Swiss lake scene, 'Someone to care for Me' in a most touching interlude with her father, and a classic aria in, of all places, a police station. Her rendering of 'Someone to care for me' has nuances of the more mature artist who gives us 'When You're Away' in 'His Butler's Sister'. In a young girl's song for the benefit of an astonished and almost mesmerised parent there is a delicate and soulfully expressed yearning for reciprocal love which becomes so articulate in the young woman of later years when the beginnings of desire compete with her ambition to impress a composer – I refer again to 'When You're Away' and the rather unsympathetic character for whom it was sung whose hearing, surprisingly enough, is so defective that he cannot co-ordinate the incidence of sound with its proper source.

The gentle and demure little lass who sings with an almost ghostly look in her eyes to a soulful-looking Charles Winnger – torn between his memories and three ravishing daughters on the one hand and a crafty socialite on the other – revealed a sensitivity in her acting which always seemed to emerge so naturally. Remember the elfin glance when she murmured, 'Tuck me in, daddy, will you?' And later, the unbelievable pathos when she sobbed in his arms before running away. She left the gloves which she always wore when worried to prevent herself from biting her nails, lying on her vacated bed like a symbol of renunciation.

What I saw in her performance was not the paid artist, nor a professional simulation, but the genuine person portraying a real human feeling. And the final shot of the film when Deanna gazes adoringly in turn at parents reunited after ten long years of separation, is a superb illustration of Deanna's ability to pull at the heartstrings. Her eyes shining with love and her glowing face so expressive of the thankfulness that fills her heart at a longed-for reconciliation (of which she has been the prime architect) were unmistakable signs of a remarkable talent and a disposition instinctively attuned to situations of tender emotion.

And I must remark, how swiftly she could transform herself into a creature of infectious gaiety. I can always recall with unstinted pleasure the sight of Penny laughing unrestrainedly on her bed, a bed which had collapsed under her father's weight and left him sprawling on the mattress in an undignified heap. He too was convulsed with laughter.

How different that bedlam must have sounded in the ears of two conspiring females in the atrium below when only a few moments before they had heard sounds which suggested Penny was on the receiving end of a hearty spanking. The scene itself seemed so natural, one forgot that actors were involved. It was certainly an instance when professional artists could be said to be enjoying their performance for its own sake. The exceptional quality which touched people's hearts when her role dictated that she show extreme distress, was manifest in this first film of Deanna's and won something bordering on encomium from film critics and audiences alike. Who might not feel the deep surge of a protective instinct towards an unhappy Penny when she slipped into her father's bedroom and wept in his arms? Her vague intimation that she would be going away on the morrow whither no one would trace her – but knowing not where, nor caring about the future with her family finally on the verge of break-up – a delicate blackmail in Penny's case, for she sensed that some extreme measures were required to change her father's mind, could be seen as the reaction of one torn by despair and tribulation. But her tears on Judson's shoulder shed by a little, lost girl who was fighting for the happiness of her absent mother, had none the less more than mere nuances of make-believe. It was no wonder that as a newcomer to the screen her performance received the accolade of words such as 'spectacular' and 'phenomenal'. And few of her admirers would dissent from such judgement.

A little girl's determination to frustrate the wiles of a gold-digger – her lively, unflagging spirit in the face of disappointment and looming calamity – the superb artistry with which she invited the observer to share her most intimate thoughts, the subtle way she inveigled 'daddy' to think seriously about the wisdom of committing himself to a woman who was both mercenary and predator in the courts of love, showing that for all her immaturity she was more than advanced in feminine intuitions – above all, that alluring innocence which girdled her like a halo – all these attributes and other brief glimpses of an adorable personality made it easy for her to be regarded as a 'fairy princess'.

C h a p t e r   3

—— ⌒⅊⌒ ——

100 Men and a Girl

Deanna Durbin's second film '100 Men and a Girl' was
distinguished by another brilliant performance by a relative
newcomer to the film industry.

As the only daughter, Patricia, of an out-of-work musician who is
also a widower she has a double burden – firstly, that of keeping
house for him in a miserable boarding house where the mistress is ever
on his trail for unpaid rent, and secondly, the self-imposed task of
finding a way out of a penurious existence. The simple answer of
course would be for her father to obtain employment as a trombone
player which is his particular vocation. Daddy, John Cardwell, as
played by the inimitable Adolphe Menjou, a gifted character actor in
his day, is in quest of such a job and makes a nuisance of himself in a
concert hall where Leopold Stokowski has just finished another
virtuoso exhibition of his art to a wildly enthusiastic audience. John is
forcibly ejected and while he is lingering disconsolately outside the
foyer he observes a purse lying on the pavement which has been
inadvertently dropped by a concert-goer and is ignored by a dispersing

crowd. He picks it up, examines the banknotes inside and stuffs it in his pocket. On his return home he is cornered by his landlady and to her astonishment hands her the rent he owes. She assumes that he has obtained the desired job with Stokowski. Almost absentmindedly he makes no attempt to correct that assumption. Patricia naturally is overjoyed and so John, despite his misgivings, accepts the congratulations of the other lodgers. To celebrate a fictitious change of fortune a party is held in the lodging-house during which Patricia sings 'It's Raining Sunbeams' – a precious jewel of a tune which gives you a vision of a dreamland where never clouds intrude.

The following day John Cardwell goes off as he pretends to rehearsal, unaware that Patricia has followed him to the concert-hall. There she has to elude a vigilant door-keeper, who naturally denies that her father is a member of the orchestra, and manages surreptitiously to get a close look at the musicians in rehearsal. There is of course no sign of her father, and that evening when he comes home from a card game saying how well the day went and how he received the congratulations of Stokowski himself for his playing, Patricia bursts into tears. She does not upbraid him unduly, however, because she senses that it was for her peace of mind in particular that he persisted in his falsehood. As is the way sometimes of a maladroit though kindly fortune, the retention of the purse gives Patricia an opportunity of correcting the situation inasmuch as it is a prelude to a chain of events which ultimately brings a change of circumstances and well-deserved happiness.

For, armed with the purse from which she has obtained the owner's address and knowing precisely just how much her father has spent of the money it contained, Patricia hurries to the home of the lady in question and to the latter's amusement and the delight of her guests insists that the reward offered her should total exactly fifty-two dollars and ten cents – the sum appropriated by her father, i.e. fifty-two dollars for rent and ten cents for coffee. She promptly returns the reward money, saying virtually that a debt has been discharged. Intrigued by her novel approach and rather whimsical morality, a swarm of socialites presses all manner of delicacies upon her at a crowded buffet, and it is unquestionably a joy to see a girl, unused to such luxuries, hardly able to make a choice at a sumptuous feast. Plied with questions about her personal life as enticing confections and savouries are heaped upon her plate she lets slip the fact that her father is a clever musician who taught her to sing. And before she can gulp a mouthful or two she is virtually bundled across the room by the hostess and her friends to a grand piano and a waiting orchestra. Nobody is expecting a performance to bring the house down, certainly not from a poor girl whose clothes are of nondescript quality – but, as you might expect, that is precisely what Deanna does with consummate ease. 'A Heart That's Free' is the song she sings and everybody is stunned by the purity of her voice which indicates an incredible talent. She is so young and yet her soprano has a maturity and range which leaves her listeners almost awe-struck. Her performance finished, Patricia prepares to satisfy her hunger, but when in a discussion on the problems of the day some wag remarks that the remedy for unemployed musicians is more orchestras, she is struck by a sudden thought. Would there be sponsorship forthcoming if her father got together an orchestra of a hundred out-of-work musicians. Says the hostess decisively to Patrician – 'You get your orchestra together and I'll sponsor it.' Patrician is thrilled and, tempting though the buffet is, she hurries off amid a gale of laughter to break the glad tidings to her father. Ah, so sweet and ingenuous is she to believe in a promise given carelessly in a delirious party atmosphere by a languid and basically uncaring hostess who is due to leave almost immediately on a jaunt to Europe and, as it transpires, her extravagant pledge forgotten.

Patricia is utterly convincing in her unique single-mindedness when she sets out to persuade a wealthy financier to delve into his bank balance and behave selflessly for once. She hurries to a gentlemen's club in the search for sponsorship by the husband of a lady who has rashly committed herself at a party to become a saviour to the unemployed. A rotund Eugene Pallette plays the role of the husband, a man given to practical joking with a colleague. He assumes that Patricia is a conspirator in a jape when she tells him about the sponsorship he is expected to undertake. He is dumb-founded at first when the truth dawns and then outraged. He refuses blankly to have anything to do with the whole proposition and so redeem his wife's promise. It is therefore not difficult to feel no sympathy at all for him when he presents himself at a garage Patricia's father has rented for rehearsal and repudiates any involvement, only to receive a buffet in the face from an angry conductor. He has his uses, however, particularly his shouted advice to a stunned orchestra that they should get some master of the baton to conduct them. The publicity deriving from such a performance could well lead to professional engagements. Listening intently to the dispute, Patricia is swift to appreciate the possibilities which might evolve from following such advice. Off she goes then, stealing out of the garage theatre-bound, thanks to the generosity of taxi-driver, Frank Jenks (policeman in 'First Love' and ardent admirer in 'His Butler's Sister').

It is easy to chuckle in retrospect when one remembers that dainty little hat with a sprouting feather which Deanna wore when she tried to slip once again unobserved into forbidden territory to contact Stokowski.

From his theatre kiosk a fat janitor stares at a feather bobbing along just above window level. He wobbles forth to discover an enterprising girl crawling along on all fours to gain unauthorised entry. The incident is repeated when she escapes his clutches and chases upstairs to the auditorium. There goes that feather again, protruding just above the chairbacks as Deanna crawls between the rows of vacant seats. Stokowski is rehearsing, oblivious of the comedy involving the janitor and an elusive girl. The humour of that situation was infinitely superior to that generated by the practical jokes of a couple of portly businessmen, notwithstanding their childish pre-disposition in this respect had a direct bearing on the plot. After the janitor has withdrawn in some despair a tense moment follows. Leopold Stokowski is about to begin conducting Mozart's 'Alleluia'. His baton falls and Deanna breaks into song immediately to the amazement of the maestro and his orchestra. But the great man carries on and seems positively to enjoy Deanna's remarkable voice in full flow.

Deanna's rendition of Mozart's 'Alleluia' in a comedy of errors ingeniously devised constitutes perhaps the most heart-warming moments of the film. Joyously she sings, even exultantly, a matchless hymn in praise of God, and though it symbolises a genuflexion to the Eternal, Deanna still contrives to give a hint of underlying diffidence in her awareness of a celebrated conductor and his company of accomplished musicians. Never did a potential prima-donna enjoy so memorable a debut in the world of grand orchestration and classic melody. The superb way in which this initiation is achieved exemplifies the masterful art of Joe Pasternak and Henry Koster. Such skills as theirs might well merit the term of 'legendary' in the sense that they succeed in tempering what might have seemed mere showmanship and sheathing the dramatic or theatrical with a mantle of simplicity. So in Deanna's acting in an imposing concert hall was projected a character too innocent to be overawed by the grandeur of any occasion, but endued with a touching humility. And perhaps that was the secret which enabled her to realise her altruistic ends.

It could be said that the role of Patricia in '100 Men and a Girl' is really a continuation of the one Deanna played in 'Three Smart Girls'. Once more she is bent on a crusade to benefit others although the objective this time is the correction of social injustice rather than the unravelling of a domestic entanglement. Once again Deanna is accompanied in this cinematic masquerade by so many supporting players who during her film career became familiar figures in the stories she brought to glowing life. The irrepressible Adolphe Menjou is ever benign though his face is too often clouded by tribulation as he gives a faultless performance as Deanna's loving father. Watching him on the screen I found it hard to reconcile his paternal stance with the middle-aged lecher of 'I'll Be Yours' so plainly bent on Deanna's seduction. I liked especially his and Deanna's reciprocal habit of pouting with smiling lips and a blink of the eyes as for instance when she is rendering 'It's Raining Sunbeams' in a moment of blissful happiness, cherishing the illusion that daddy has been given a job in Leopold Stokowski's orchestra. This little quirk is repeated by father and daughter in the closing sequence of the film when Patricia sings

'La Traviata' before a vast concert audience. Stokowski has just
conducted the orchestra of unemployed musicians, having changed his
mind since hearing them play in his own home where they were
smuggled in by a very resourceful Patricia. How joyful and proud they
all were on that occasion as they lined up on the stairs and landings in
a huge mansion while their conductor put them through their paces.
Such a venue was an inspired choice. Anyway, in the finale father is
ecstatic about Patricia's singing and as he wrinkles his nose, filial love
and affection irradiate her face as she responds. And I suppose one
must not fail to mention the presence in the orchestra of a close friend
who loves Patricia in his own way as much as her father. That part is
played by Mischa Auer, the bibulous Hungarian count of 'Three Smart
Girls', and now an absent-minded trombone-player babbling with those
sonorous vowels of his which were a fair indication of his East
European origins.

Deanna Durbin, Adolphe Menjou and Mischa Auer in '100 Men and a Girl'.
(Reproduced courtesy of The Movie Store Collection)

25

A distinctive feature of Deanna's acting in the film is the swiftness of her transition from demureness to fiery expostulation – for instance, when she rebukes an orchestra she deems unfeeling in its attitude. For who can forget that scene when full of indignation she berates Stokowski's professionals who laugh derisively as she reveals that her out-of-work musicians hold their rehearsals in a local garage, not too far away from the concert-hall in a physical sense but a far cry from the opulence and splendour of their own cavernous amphitheatre.

One final word to demonstrate how well Deanna could combine comedy with pathos. I refer to one particular sequence when she returns home after singing 'Alleluia'. Despite his tribute to her remarkable voice and his sympathy for her troubled family and friends, Stokowski explains that he is off to honour European engagements and cannot possibly conduct her orchestra before his departure. She cries brokenly in daddy's arms, at last convinced that all her efforts have been in vain. 'Why does everyone laugh at me?' she asks, and, still sobbing, continues, 'I only wanted us to have money again so you can have turkey on your birthday instead of beans.'

Tragi-comedy of a superlative kind – thanks to Deanna.

—— ୬ᢗ ᒐ ——

Mad about Music

I f it is accepted that a true fairy-tale needs a backdrop of mighty mountains, brooding forests and limpid lakes to give it an aura of realism, then the film 'Mad About Music', Deanna Durbin's third, could only have been set in a country like Switzerland to project the illusion – a picturesque excursion into fantasy – a dream-world 'ancient as the hills of Xanadu', to warm the jaded heart and to excite the credulous. 'Mad About Music' does indeed generate that fairy-tale atmosphere. Its opening sequence in a Swiss panorama is an instant reminder of 'Three Smart Girls'. A group of pretty schoolgirls nearing graduation age, cycling merrily along country lanes in Maytime, in a blur of springtime blossom and mellifluous song, has its counterpart in the previous film in a lake scene with a small, sailing craft skimming through placid waters and a young girl singing in the stern. Both episodes are evocative enough of hope as well as youth as to brighten the most jaundiced eye.

‘Mad About Music’ is the story of a fatherless youngster at school in Switzerland, separated for years from her mother who is a successful film actress in the United States and who, in order to maintain her glamorous image as a movie star, is obliged to eschew all contact with her teenage daughter. It is more than a challenging role for a budding actress about that age but through all the ramifications of a heart-warming tale Deanna preserved credibility as one who has been ostracised as it were through no fault of her own and is pining for parental love and affection.

All who admire and love Deanna and who have enjoyed her films will be familiar with the plot – an unwitting composer taking a short vacation in Switzerland is drawn into a delightful conspiracy with a sweet and attractive girl. He plays the part of a 'mythical' father, honorary explorer, if the term is permissible, until the denouement in Paris establishes as it were his legitimacy in respect of fatherhood, and enables him for good measure to acquire a very appealing wife. But there will be many who may have forgotten some of the detail – the incidental sequences which in retrospect revive in a lively way the pleasure they kindled on their first showing. Poignancy too when Deanna reacted tearfully to difficulties which at the time seemed insuperable. Rather impulsively she has hinted that her father is passing through the area by train, and the news electrifies both her classmates and the school governess, for hitherto the only proof of his existence has been a series of letters which Deanna has written herself and got the school caretaker and handyman to transcribe.

One can imagine the utter misery and sense of hopelessness she felt when she was awaiting the arrival of a train supposedly bringing her father to glad reunion with his offspring. There she stood on a railway platform watched closely by her schoolfriends all eager for their first glimpse of a bold explorer (an occupation invented by Deanna to account for his protected absence). She was clutching a bouquet of flowers which she had previously tossed into the hands of a railway porter when she thought she was unobserved and hurriedly snatched back when she became aware of the presence of a babbling, goggling crowd of classmates. Hopefully but on the brink of despair Deanna eyed the passengers descending from the train. Whom should she approach as a likely father with a pretended word of endearment on her lips, perhaps even an embrace. The welcome had to seem realistic under the keen scrutiny of precocious teenagers who were not easily to be bamboozled.

Having at last accosted a very startled composer played by Herbert Marshall, who is accompanied by a rather aggressive manservant, Deanna becomes inventive about a Swiss custom of welcoming distinguished strangers and whisks both men away to a horse-drawn carriage parked conveniently nearby.

Deanna's anxieties do not diminish, however. Her arch-enemy at school, a little vixen played by Helen Parrish, is far from convinced that the 'explorer', so fortuitously come to Deanna's rescue, is her genuine father, and still driven by an unreasoning dislike of the hotel where the two visitors will be staying. One moment Deanna is leaning forward into a lift in pretence of embracing her 'father' – the next she glimpses her tormentor on the point of hurrying to the reception desk to determine if she can establish daddy's real identity. If her suspicions are correct he will be registered under a different name to that of the schoolgirl whose father he is supposed to be. But Deanna's reaction is swift as she dashes across the entrance hall, brushes her enemy aside and audibly to others reminds the reception clerk that her father is travelling incognito. By such expediency does she preserve at least temporarily her precious dream that in common with her class mates she does indeed have a father who loves and cherishes her.

Underlying the droll comedy of those memorable sequences in a delightful fairy-tale there is the pathos of an adorable and very sensitive young lass almost at her wits end in her efforts to avoid the ignominy of being exposed as a cheat or a fraud for all that her motives are entirely selfless. Deanna excelled in the art of displaying conflicting emotions, the air of one startled almost to the point of distraction when faced by sudden calamity and desperately seeking a way out of a dilemma. Remember her in 'Nice Girl'? – the man with whom she had supposedly spent a night of lust and whom she claimed she was to marry? He made an unexpected appearance at a party where she was receiving congratulations on her engagement. There was the prospect of her having to face contempt and derision should he pour scorn on her pretensions. One quick sideways toss of the head in search of immediate salvation was all she needed to express her panic. (Sometimes a prompt departure is the only alternative to having the ground open beneath the feet to escape acute embarrassment, if nothing worse.)

'Mad about Music' is a film rich in instances where comedy is derived solely from the supposed naiveté of the performers, as at the dinner given by the headmistress of Deanna's school in honour of a distinguished and intrepid explorer. In her bogus father Deanna found a willing if not altogether convincing accomplice in maintaining the fiction of a close relationship. One would expect any composer of mild temperament and aesthetic tastes, regular in his habits perhaps and too well bred to behave unconventionally, to be at a loss when suddenly called upon to make the transition to a man of action, alert, masterful, swift in his response to danger and above all never lacking in courage and resource. It would be difficult for such a one to live up to the extravagant image invoked by an imaginative daughter to impress her hearers before his appearance on the scene. Herbert Marshall's attempts to sound credible as the character in question might well be called hilarious. But when I first saw the film I did not mind in the least his absurd patter about his exploits as a big-game hunter. For the lovely Gloria (to give Deanna her real name in the script) was close at his side prompting him and ensuring with timely interventions that the barrage of questions and comments directed at him from all sides did not lead him into error or mis-judgement and raise doubts as to his integrity. But far from being discomfited he entered into the spirit of things and even surprised Gloria with his fable of a mysterious 'white queen' whose sanctuary he sought in the deepest jungle. Purists and realists, if not the more sceptical among humans, might well dismiss such romanticism as ridiculous, more suited to a juvenile fancy. And the more informed might judge his ignorance about tropical fauna to be abysmal. But I am sure the director of the film was no ignoramus and simply wished to present the whole episode as good and wholesome fun. It was my impression anyway that those fortunate enough to see 'Mad About Music' when it appeared in the cinema in those days of long ago thoroughly enjoyed Marshall's verbal antics. They generated laughter, not derision or embarrassment. Apart from the fantasy about a white queen of the jungle there were other fatuities to convulse anyone with a facile sense of humour, such as his dissertation involving elephants. 'I looked the elephant in the eye and he knew that I was his master' – then, in response to query, this pearl of wisdom – 'You can only look at one eye at a time because they are situated on either side of his head'. But such idiocies are easily forgivable when attention is focused on the bewitching Gloria seated on his right, deliciously happy that the masquerade seems to be continuing without a hitch. By contrast with such pantomime, Deanna Durbin and Herbert Marshall were at their very best when playing several touching scenes together.

After the banquet in his honour we find the bogus father conversing seriously in Gloria's study at the school while she talks about her family background and seeks to explain her motives for pretending that her father is an explorer of some note. She tells him about her deceased father and decides to show him photographs of her parents.

There followed one of the most emotive scenes Deanna ever played in any of her films – extremely plaintive in a sense and touching enough perhaps to bring a sympathetic tear even to the unsentimental eye. Gloria's initial hesitancy as she goes to a bureau is that of a girl who is torn between growing trust in a good Samaritan and doubt of the propriety of unveiling to a stranger's gaze intimate mementoes of her personal life. The look of amusement and compassion on the bogus father's face as he watches Gloria unlocking a drawer in the bureau, taking forth a key, then unlocking a second drawer to remove a casket from which she extracts another key, this one the means of unlocking the drawer in another cabinet to locate at last her precious photographs, is fully expressive of the tenderness, if not a fatherly kind of love, he feels for her. And while he scans a picture of her mother clasping a baby Gloria in her arms, he is not unconscious of a lustrous tear shimmering in the eyes of the girl beside him. Assuredly one can be forgiven for thinking that such situations, however competent or inspired the performance or sensitive the director, owe less to the histrionic art than the qualities of heart and mind necessary to enhance the imagery. The inference must be that those involved are themselves persons of rare goodwill and fine sensitivity.

Following the emotional interlude in Gloria's study there are several sequences of fun and fraternisation in which the explorer-parent is accepted as something like a patriarch in a scholastic community. The frolics are suspended when he is summoned away on business and there is another moving moment when he and Gloria say farewell. He is bound for Paris and when by a coincidence a newspaper headline announces the arrival of Gloria's mother – now hailed as a glamorous filmstar – from America to attend a celebrity function in the French capital, Gloria sees it as an ideal opportunity of making contact with a loved one she has not seen for many years. The next glimpse of Gloria is the diverting spectacle of an anxious teenager tearing along the corridor of a moving train chased by an incensed ticket collector who believes she is attempting to travel without paying her fare to Paris. She on the other hand is simply searching for her bogus father to attend to that matter but is forced eventually to sing at the top of her voice to attract his attention. And so to Paris and the hotel where her mother is staying, only to be reminded by the manager of that film star that if it is discovered that a very glamorous person has a fourteen-year-old daughter the consequent publicity is likely to damage a promising career. Gloria therefore keeps quiet about an intimate relationship although she is heart-broken at having to leave without contacting her mother. The intervention of a shrewd composer is required to reunite Gloria and her mother. The final scene with a happy teenager singing a reprise of 'Serenade to the Stars' while film star and composer hold hands confirms our view that Gloria will not be fatherless much longer in the conventional sense of the word.

It seems almost irrelevant to add that 'Mad About Music' provides further confirmation, if that were needed, of Deanna Durbin's remarkable talents as an actress. And when such a one who is a combination of youthful charm and bewitching appeal has also the providential gift of a singing voice of the rarest quality, one can only despair of finding the correct terminology to do justice to her singularity. When, as in this film, she is singing an aria like Gounod's 'Ava Maria' from an oratorio of renown, or the dreamy stanzas of 'Chapel Bells' or the romantic 'Serenade to the Stars', I can only hold my breath and lose myself in the rapture of her voice, the sheer wonder of it all. I say quite unashamedly that in the Thirties and Forties I came to look upon Deanna Durbin as a kind of goddess who ruled my imaginary self. Every film of her I saw was refreshment of that subconscious dream. As the years flew by after her departure from Hollywood it was but rarely the opportunity came of watching any of the films she made during her brief career. But always the memory of those early days was for me, and doubtless a nameless host around the globe, something sweet and timeless. Her lovely, wistful face and enchanting voice was always an elixir to those legions of worshippers world-wide. Despite the depredations of time I am sure those original legions are not disbanded. Some of us still survive, thank heaven, to recall that dreamtime, a time of 'putting hearts together' of which Deanna sang in a later film 'I'll Be yours'. And it is a joy to know that the goddess herself is with us still – she shines in our hearts and in our minds. One does not think of time bearing her in its flow to that confluence with destiny which soon or late engulfs us all. For Deanna symbolises for me and those who feel as I do a religion which is ageless, a gospel of love and joy, of youth indestructible, above all of innocence – an everlasting kaleidoscope in which all the reflections are bright and beautiful. There are no words which may truly unravel the depth of feeling she inspired, and still does, in those who love the image she created, I do not doubt, unwittingly. Finally, can I forbear to say that Springtime like a dancing nymph is the shadow at her heel?

Chapter 5

That Certain Age

The title of Deanna's next film, 'That Certain Age', bespeaks the kind of juvenile romanticism embodied in the script. Deanna has the name of Alice bestowed upon her in this comedy of adolescent affection and love, and she really is engulfed in a wonderland of light intrigue. She has a very shy boy friend, Ken, aged sixteen or thereabouts, competently played by Jackie Cooper, and a mother and father who prove to be not too bright when it comes to pointing a daughter in the right direction in respect of her romantic attachments. Her father, a press baron, invites Vincent, a prominent war correspondent, to his country mansion for a rest and recuperation prior to his leaving on another assignment abroad. Vincent, as one might expect, is sophisticated, worldly-wise and more than twice Deanna's age, more concerned with his creature comforts than amorous dalliance.

The invitation entails Alice and her friends of both sexes giving up an apartment which has been the venue for their musical plays and light operas. Alice and her companions therefore plot to get rid of him, or lest this phrase be considered as a euphemism for something criminal, make his stay so miserable as to drive him away. Accordingly they devise all manner of deterrents to induce the unwitting guest to leave. At first the rather crude expedient of tormenting him with pellets from a pea-shooter is employed amid talk of mosquitoes and the 'like'. Then a bunch of resourceful youngsters tries to make him believe that his apartment is haunted. Articles of furniture and other artefacts move about, seemingly of their own volition, or perhaps there are poltergeists materialising unseen in dark corners to project this illusion of the supernatural at work. With not too much difficulty Vincent discovers these are tricks being played upon him and to the surprise and pleasure of Alice and her friends assures them that he will be glad to leave. (Vincent of course is a thoroughly urbanised creature and the smell of new-mown hay is anathema to him.) He is very ready therefore to co-operate in any scheme which will facilitate his departure. Capriciously, however, Alice develops a crush on him and does her utmost to thwart a plan collectively agreed. She appears to lose all interest in the lovesick Ken as well as theatrical activities as she concentrates her attention on Vincent. Her infatuation is such that she pawns many of the baubles hoarded during her childhood and even a treasured bicycle in order to purchase a watch for him as a gift. The sacrifice also enables her to have an inscription engraved on the watch which is virtually an avowal of her love for him. At a party she sings soulfully the song 'My Own' while he unwraps her gift. In desperation Vincent, who has affection for Alice but no reciprocal feelings of adoration or love, turns for help to her parents. At all costs she must be discouraged. Their heart-to-heart talks with their daughter fail abysmally and Vincent has to conjure up a wife whose arrival in the household convinces Alice of Vincent's duplicity. A disillusioned young girl transfers her affection back to an astonished but delighted Ken. He is head-over-heels in love with her and when she rejoins the young community and the cast of a musical play he is exuberant in his relief and joy. A ballet-like skip testifies to his jubilation. When she sings the Waltz Song from Romeo and Juliet in a grand finale he becomes almost incoherent with delight and worship of his dream-girl. The sight of that homage is good to behold as well as understanding of emotions which we, the audience, can most heartily approve.

What further comment can one make on 'That Certain Age'? Doubtless in every age, in every clime since the human story began, the very young and adolescent (feminine gender) have both expressed and survived a brief period of infatuation with males older than themselves, indeed, even those teetering on the brink of middle age. So there is nothing phenomenal in such obsession; it can be a theme for comedy or burlesque and is often so treated. And thus it is in this light-hearted tale with Deanna playing the part of a love-sick adolescent. Perhaps her co-star, however, might have been more responsive to her provocative charm. He stands so aloof at times from a picturesque charade with an air of almost cynical amusement as he contemplates the antics and assesses the thought processes of youngsters with whom he has little in common. There is more than a touch of condescension in his manner when he professes interest in their activities and preoccupations. He still maintains a puzzled detachment even when there are clear signs that an impressionable girl, flitting about him with thoughts of a demi-god and a soulful yearning in her eyes, is plainly thinking of entrusting her future to his care. I think that Melvyn Douglas as Vincent lacked the sensitivity which Walter Pidgeon displayed in 'It's a Date' when he too became companion to a delightful stranger.

And this leads me to wonder whether it was by chance or design that in several of her roles it was Deanna who first had to indicate her love for another, acting with partners who seemed initially insensible to her charms. Why did she have to do the chasing instead of being eagerly pursued? I grant you there were exceptions – Adolphe Menjou, for instance, in 'I'll Be Yours', but he was driven by improper motives as was the lecherous producer in 'His Butler's Sister', the one who was going to teach her 'perse'. Even in 'Hers to Hold' she had to avow herself enamoured of a conceited young aviator more priapic than virtuous. Again in 'The Amazing Mrs Holliday' Deanna had to reveal her true feelings, if only to a perceptive Timothy, before her eventual betrothed was ready to declare his love for her. And I can only repeat, bearing in mind Deanna's charm and grace, that it would have been more realistic to have cast her in the role of being desired before desiring, purely as a preliminary to a closer liaison; I would have preferred her partners to have been in no way constrained but demonstrative enough to have fallen at her feet in silent worship.

Deanna Durbin and Melvyn Douglas in 'That Certain Age'.
(Reproduced courtesy of The Movie Store Collection)

I found the surrogate Deanna Durbin of the cinema screen in all her moods to be ever alluring. She kindled the emotions, some indefinable, which have much to do with the refinement of the human spirit and nothing relating to its darker images. Her infectious gaiety, never wholly suppressed by the doubts and uncertainties her role called for, had a dreamlike quality which was irresistible and sometimes her bewitching smile of dawning revelation chasing away some perplexity or disbelief was rapture to behold. It suffused her face and enhanced her loveliness.

Though it is almost a cliché to say that some particular film was further evidence of the remarkable acting ability of one so young as Deanna, it is nevertheless true of 'That Certain Age'. And incontrovertible truth it is. The maturity of her unique soprano when she sang the Waltz Song from Romeo and Juliet and 'My Own' made me reflect that such quality like the instrument itself are gifts rarely bestowed by a benign Providence on aspiring mortals. I reflect too how splendidly fortuitous it is that in respect of Deanna herself a marvellous technology (so timely in the field of human progress) enables such gifts to become a source of immense pleasure to millions world-wide. What a blessing this great artist was not born in a previous century when there were no means of perpetuating glorious sound for the benefit of future generations. And to pursue the analogy on a more personal basis, at the risk once more of repeating the sentiment, I count myself lucky to be part of a world in which the living Deanna sang to enchant the ear and the eye and to enrich the spirit. All of which perhaps has no direct relevance to the plot and the performance of individual players in 'That Certain Age' itself. Suffice to say that the film more than enhanced Deanna's reputation as an actress of considerable versatility and a singer with few, if any, to rival her for sentimental charm and virtuosity.

Chapter 6

Three Smart Girls Grow up

'Three Smart Girls Grow Up', Deanna Durbin's fifth major film, released just before the outbreak of the war of 1939, is a sequel to the first film which she made that was so sensational in its impact on the cinema-going public – not least the acclaim with which it was greeted by the film industry itself and critics in the entertainment and journalistic world. It was a continuation of the saga of the Craig family.

In the very opening scene we are given no reason to doubt that affairs of the heart, the young heart, so capricious but so sincere, will become the dominating theme of perhaps the happiest film Deanna made, gloomy incidents included. Her Penny Craig is just a more adult version of the loveable character, always in surroundings of elegance and refinement reflecting the family's social status and wealth. She is invariably wearing beautiful clothes and her whole aspect is of womanly grace allied with a real measure of self-assurance in her dealings with her two older sisters. In marked contrast they seem constantly to be in considerable doubt of their probable future and the fruition of their desires in the area of love and romance. The eldest, Joan, becomes engaged to a suave and good-looking young man named Richard although neither of the twain is really in love with the other. But their ultimate union in wedlock is regarded almost as a *fait accompli* by both friends and relatives so that the couple begin to feel that they should do what is expected of them – continue their association in a convincing way and marry. Only Penny comes to realise that her other sister, Kay, is secretly in love with Joan's fiancé when in the 'still of the night' she awakes to find Kay's bed empty and steals up on her silently in an adjoining room where Kay is in some distress. She is weeping over her diary of which Penny, craning her neck in a chamber lit only by firelight, gets only a fleeting glimpse or two. But she reads enough to learn the truth about Kay's feelings before her sister with a sob of renunciation tosses her diary into the fire. Penny steals back to bed before Kay can discover her presence. Thereafter Penny concentrates on finding a suitable young man, inevitably tall, dark and handsome, to win Kay's heart – someone anyway who will help her to forget Richard, a young man already committed to the matrimonial couch. Fate is perverse, however, for the one she chooses who conforms to the conventional image she has in mind (the role here is admirably filled by Robert Cummings as Harry Loren) promptly shows more interest in Joan. Penny's impatience with him, frustration even, is wrongly construed by her sisters and parents as jealousy on her part. Ridiculous though such an idea is to Penny, it is nevertheless treated seriously by the Craig family, Penny's mother in particular. As a consequence the youngest Craig is barred by her parents from further training at the music academy where she is studying so that she may be denied further contact with Harry who works in an a joining studio at the school. Bereft of ideas as well as hope, Penny turns to her father in some despair and invades his office to enact a very tender scene of 'little girl lost'. In response to Penny's accusation that he never seems to have time to listen to his daughter's troubles, her father, Judson Craig, says that it is because he must work to provide for his daughters and give them the things they need. Penny's tearful retort is memorable – 'We don't want things, daddy –

we just want love and understanding – someone who will listen to us when we are unhappy'. Poor daddy does listen for once and takes all his telephones off the hook in order to do so without interference from that imperious contraption. Later he acts decisively at Joan's wedding ceremony to ensure the future happiness of his two senior daughters. He delivers Joan into the arms of Harry who is not an official guest. Then he leads Kay, the substitute bride to take her place beside an astonished but delighted Richard. On her father's arm, bound for the altar, Kay gives Penny a look of undying gratitude, knowing well the one who is responsible for making her dreams come true. As for Penny – her time will come when she meets an intrepid but incorrigible aviator in 'Hers To Hold'.

In general comment on 'Three Smart Girls Grow Up' I think it is implicit in the title that three young ladies in question will become romantically involved. That was true of course in respect of the two elder daughters. And it was wise to keep Penny, the youngest of the trio, free of such emotional entanglement. Casting her in the role of matchmaker was an inspired move. The confusion, heartache and recrimination involving the whole Craig family is, we suspect, never too serious, but well demonstrated by a superb cast. That Penny's laudable and unselfish motives in seeking to ensure her sisters' future happiness should be misconstrued by the persons involved, including her parents, is a circumstance on which the plot hangs. It was not true to character, however, that her mother should behave in a rather obtuse fashion. She is after all a senior member of a sex reputedly perceptive and shrewd in matters of the heart. Her irascibility and unfeeling abruptness of manner towards Penny seemed to indicate that she had forgotten that it was her youngest daughter's remarkable insight and initiative which brought about a reconciliation with a long absent spouse. A concerned and sensible mother in real life would assuredly have asked herself why Penny was behaving in an unusual way, not told her dismissively after one altercation to go to her room. The least observant in a cinema audience would be well aware that Penny was the wisest of them all because unlike others her wisdom came from her heart and not her intellect.

41

Deanna Durbin, Nan Grey and Helen Parrish in 'Three Smart Girls Grow up'.
(Reproduced courtesy of The Movie Store Collection)

In such an emotional atmosphere one can forgive the male head of the household who has a memory like a sieve, is incoherent most of the time and preoccupied with his business affairs, invariably conducted by long distance telephone, to the exclusion of all else, especially his home life. One also feels sorry for Penny in her repeated but vain attempts to engage his attention long enough to explain the predicament threatening the welfare of his offspring – and tends to curse the telephone which always rings at a crucial moment to draw him away and leave Penny forlorn and despairing. It is not before time that he comes to his senses and listens earnestly to Penny's tale of woe. He is deservedly upbraided by her and when she weeps copiously he becomes at last aware of his own insensitivity. Deanna's emotional 'tour de force' in a company boardroom is unforgettable, being ineffably touching and true as ever was life in the real world. Such a beautiful, if tearful, picture of profound despair, of hopeless longing and pathetic resignation, was she in that scene – not a blemish in her acting. Her father rightly cradles her in his arms and whispers words of consolation and reassurance that all would ultimately end well. And indeed it did, in that astonishing and rather ingenious switch of brides at a wedding ceremony. Whoever heard of a father giving away his daughter by leading her away from the altar where the bridegroom was waiting, to commit her to the care of another lover waiting outside the church? Craig senior proved in that magnificent denouement that business acumen was not his sole talent and its function the prime purpose of his existence.

In this film Deanna demonstrates how far she has progressed in her acting from the time of 'Three Smart Girls' when her tutelage was entrusted to an enlightened producer named Pasternak. He turned an inexperienced girl into a more than competent actress whose delightful and vivacious personality and intelligence assuredly made the transition easier. And in 'Three Smart Girls Grow Up' all the original qualities of her first screen appearance are very markedly still there – the charming demeanour, an unfailing freshness and grace, the underlying blend of ready sympathy and an irrepressible sense of fun; the wistfulness moreover when, as Shakespeare said, 'the world is too much with us', and her thoughts are troublous. Anyway, to saddle a young girl with the task of assuring that her two sisters should make the right choice in respect of their future husbands was the sort of commission to unnerve grown men and women wisest in understanding of human nature and its fluctuating moods. Deanna had so many mannerisms which, shall we say, were not necessarily part of 'stage repertoire', that every scene in which she appeared was touched with a hint of magic and mystery, whether they told of resolve tinged with doubt, hope combined with fear, or an inner strength that did not disguise a sense of fragility and innocence. There was a modesty too, rare in that one felt it was a natural manifestation, not something contrived or artificial.

In this superb film Deanna sings several songs in magnificent style. One adapted from Weber's Invitation to the Waltz is a poetic dream. Never did the bell-like quality of a unique voice reveal itself with such masterful ease or perfection. A veritable cascade of thrilling notes set the nerve ends tingling. And how angelic was her composure when she sang that wonderful Irish song, 'Last Rose of Summer' in response to her father's wish, though clearly she was wondering what had prompted such a request at an unwonted hour, approaching bedtime. So enraptured was he, nevertheless, that he had clearly forgotten the ruse his wife had planned to prevent Penny returning to a local academy of music. How genuine seemed Penny's disillusion when her troubled sire brusquely told her that her voice was awful and that further instruction at school would be a waste of time. Frankly I found this a bit unbelievable. Loving parents do not behave so churlishly. Nor can I image them believing the fiction that their daughter might be in love with somebody she had lately called a nincompoop for thwarting her plans.

That perennial masterpiece, 'Because', psalm and hymn to all who love pure and unsophisticated melody rather than dramatic operatic effusions, brought 'Three Smart Girls Grow Up' to a grand finale as Penny's two sisters swapped partners under the direction of their father. Deanna's singing had the greatest emotional impact in a chaotic scene of changing allegiances, bewildered looks and anxious murmurings; and a final shot of an ecstatic songstress pouring forth a rich libation of song in the fullness of her heart.

Never was anthem more beautifully sung to soften the discord in the human heart or to serve as balm upon its contradictions.

Chapter 7

─── ⌒⊱⊰⌒ ───

First Love

eanna's sixth film, released shortly after the outbreak of war in
1939 was unfortunately not made in colour, a circumstance
which I can only lament since it might have transformed the traditional
ballroom scene which is the highlight of any tale based on the legend
of Cinderella as this story is. Although Deanna is unbelievably demure,
almost angelic, in her role. I cannot but feel her appearance would
have been enhanced to a more fascinating degree with the advantage
of colour, perhaps the softer and more delicate hues rather than the
vivid tints within the spectrum. They would certainly have unveiled in
a more positive way those glorious blue eyes as was done in 'Can't
Help Singing', the only film, alas, that she made in colour.

The film, 'First Love' is the story of a girl named Connie,
orphaned at an early age, whose schooling and musical studies are
paid for by a gruff but kindly uncle to whose home in New York she
goes to live after graduation. She becomes embroiled in the emotional
affairs of a very selfish and self-centred cousin (Barbara) who treats her
despicably and despises her for her familiarity with the servants of the

household. They love Connie as much for her sweet and timorous disposition as her delightful singing. Naturally in this recreation of the Cinderella tale, albeit a modernised version, the most impressive sequence unfolds in a grand ballroom of sumptuous decor, aglow everywhere with festive light – jewels bedecking lovely women flashing like the crystal chandeliers overhead in the light of the lamps.

At this lavish function Connie seizes the opportunity to sing and literally becomes the 'belle of the ball'. And it is in the midst of this opulent and privileged gathering that she really meets for the first time the 'prince' she has long dreamed about, recognising him from a previous but fleeting encounter. He has ambitions of travelling abroad, ostensibly to prove that he can survive without the patronage of his wealthy father. Not surprisingly all these aspirations vanish in the spell which Connie casts upon him. He basks in her smile and seems willing to become her slave – who wouldn't? As in the original story Cinderella Connie vanishes from the ball at midnight. In Connie's case her disappearance involves an escape to the tranquillity of the country and the academy of her former governess. This flight is the consequence of an ugly sister (Barbara) contriving her utmost to destroy an innocent girl's dream. She is pursued to this rural retreat by her prince, holding as you can guess, needlessly for the purpose of recognition and more in conformity with the legend than the requirements of the plot, the dainty slipper which Connie has left behind on a stairway when she raced homeward from the ball mindful of the midnight deadline on her attendance. All very predictable but none the less entertaining. Result – reunion with a loved one and roses all the way, the film fading out with the final caption -'They lived happily ever after'. You would expect nothing less, but it is nevertheless a wistful tale in a contemporary masquerade – incredibly moving too at times thanks to Deanna's tenderly sensitive portrayal of the principal character,

In this amusing foray as in so many of her films the dresses worn by Deanna were beautifully designed and cut. Their discreet opulence seemed to emphasise the attractiveness of the wearer. Delicately coiffured on formal occasions, she was a veritable picture of elegance and refinement and sometimes the absence of jewellery save perhaps a necklace clinging unobtrusively to the soft curve of her throat, enhanced her loveliness. Nor must I forget to add that a shapely figure contributed much to her overall charm.

Deanna Durbin and Robert Stack in 'Nice Girl?'.
(Reproduced courtesy of The Aquarius Library)

So in 'First Love' when Deanna was finally dressed for the ball her aspect was dreamlike. When she pinned on an orchid, modestly refusing to give credence to a chauffeur's suggestion that it must have been sent by an admirer, that decorative flower added a perfect touch both to her costume and the adorable person sheathed in it. And you could well forgive the joy and excitement in her which impelled her to give gratuitous but nevertheless friendly advice to the objectionable Barbara and provoking the resentful retort – 'Who does she think she is – patronising me?' But still bubbling with anticipation of a wonderful evening and the possibility of meeting again the prince she has long dreamed of, Connie (the Cinderella of the film) eases herself into an expensive wrap, an all enveloping mantle of the whitest fur imaginable like a halo round her head, and an accessory on loan from an exclusive fashion house. Accordingly when Connie entered the vast mansion which was the venue for the ball she was a splendid sight in all her finery. And one can only comment again what a pity it was that the cinema screen in those far-off days of the Thirties was too often a canvas of negative black and white and intermediate shades of grey. The settings in 'First Love' which were impressive but not startling would have softened perspectives which were as uniform as they were austere and accentuated the detail. All scenes which were merely evocative might have been more than memorable for the thoughts and perhaps the imagery which colour would undoubtedly have inspired.

In the preamble to this discursive survey of an enticing world of make-believe, I referred to the effortless way in which Deanna sang. In 'First Love' her performance in respect of two notable arias was nothing less than splendid, glorious but never obtrusive. How soft was her voice, then all at once lilting, how subtle the fluctuations of sound, the marvellous crescendo which climaxed with a sustained and pulsing note! At the risk of repeating myself I must emphasise that there were never any agonised contortions of the features so often typical of those who have neither her quality of tone nor the range of octaves and have literally to bawl as they strive to reach an intensity of vocal expression which Nature did not endow them for. Deanna's singing was without strain and exquisitely controlled. As she sang, her demeanour was invariably calm, never cold, vivacious more that impassioned. She was indeed a dream figure from head to foot, glowing with tenderness and appeal. Truly in the throes of delicious song there was none to rival her.

No criticism of 'First Love' would be adequate without some reference to a few incidents which leave as lasting a memory perhaps as the more spectacular scenes depicting crowds and celebrations, rejoicing and adulation. For a start, in the opening scene with the graduation ceremony over, Connie is bustled to a piano by her school friends, all urging her to sing for them before the school disperses. And she chooses the lovely ballad, 'Home, Sweet Home'. When she breaks down before finishing the song and, overcome with emotion, sobs into her folded arms, the elderly, and forthright, principal of the establishment enquires rather brusquely, 'What's all this, then?' Connie lifts a tear-stained face, saying simply, 'Everybody's going home – I'm leaving mine.' Simple – over-sentimental? Perhaps. But Deanna as Connie caught in a very miserable moment was faultless in that portrayal.

Another instance is provided by Connie's spontaneous conversation with a very intelligent quadruped. Following an orphan girl's installation in her new home in New York her first mission is on behalf of her cousin, Barbara. Connie must detain Barbara's chosen heart-throb at an equestrian club until her cousin's arrival. To this end she pretends to be a stewardess at the club and calls for the young man in question, a rich socialite named Drake, to answer a supposed telephone call, and meanwhile tries to coax his horse away from the vicinity, filling her handbag with sugar for that purpose. 'Shamrock' the horse is a gorgeous creature who nods his head vigorously and affirmatively when she asks him if he likes sugar. He follows his temptress readily until his owner intervenes. In the subsequent action Connie is rescued by Drake from charging horses and is dazed from a fall, yet a jealous Barbara, arriving suddenly and seeing Connie reclining in her rescuer's arms, takes over from him and while he dashes away to fetch a tumbler of water she releases a fainting Connie very abruptly from her grasp. Connie falls flat on her back and bumps her head. No sympathy in the surly Barbara. Many a cinemagoer must have winced to see that very realistic jolt and watch Deanna rubbing her bruised temples.

Deanna could express astonishment with such natural innocence – well illustrated by her reaction when an aunt and cousins are discussing a ball they are shortly to attend. 'What will you wear,

Connie?' asks her male cousin unexpectedly as the girl in question is moving away despondently feeling the conversation does not involve her.

The said Connie turns abruptly, her eyes wide with wonderment. 'Oh, I'm not really going – am I?' she gulps. And when the realisation dawns that she will indeed be bound for a grand party notwithstanding Barbara's instant objection, you can almost feel her unbounded pleasure and growing excitement as she races away upstairs to ferret out the graduation dress she proposes to convert for possible evening wear.

Two other incidents to treasure follow close on her return home after a wonderful evening dancing with young Drake, her chosen prince. When she enters the hall there is a joyous greeting from the servants of the household who love her for her gentle, unselfish ways and her sweet disposition. She babbles excitedly about the events of the night, sings a bar or two of the waltz-song which left entranced her fellow guests at the ball, until her grumpy old guardian emerges from his study to complain about the noise which is interrupting his paperwork. To placate him Connie follows him into his den where she learns that he is well aware of what is going on in his house, the selfishness of his own kin, especially that of the intractable Barbara. Full of gratitude and relief to find him so understanding as well as conciliatory, Connie moves slightly forward towards his desk, her arms half extended as if she would embrace him. That instinctive but almost imperceptible urge to demonstrate her deep affection for a rather unprepossessing benefactor, conveyed in a subtle and appealing manner, hailed an actress of surpassing skill or intuition. Equally subtle was the direction of the waltz sequence with Connie and her Prince Charming totally absorbed in each other. I liked the way the ballroom was cleared of all couples save the two lovers. They danced oblivious of their surroundings in a seemingly empty ballroom, the illusion emphasising in an ingenious way that they had eyes only for each other, that they were in their own private dreamland. Eventually they move on to the terrace to seal their love with a kiss. And when they disengage Connie shyly toys with her necklace. Midnight comes,

Connie flees the ball, leaving one dainty slipper on the magnificent stairway while upstairs the ballroom is filled with dancing couples again, once more part of the real world – no longer untenanted in a dream, the magic flown.

Lasting memories I retain too, of the roar of a modernistic motor-cycle escort instead of a horse and carriage to take Connie to the ball – of house servants scattering in all directions when the odious Barbara comes bursting in to ascertain whether Connie had been to the party in defiance of her wishes – and finally the ending of the film with Deanna singing 'One Fine Day' from Madame Butterfly at her thrilling best. A small concert-hall at Connie's old school is filled with elderly spinsters, either members of the staff or having some previous connection with the academy. All the dear ladies are unashamedly weeping. Having given in Connie's missing slipper by way of identification, Connie's Prince Charming makes a smiling entrance. It is a moving scene particularly in respect of a coterie of tearful geriatrics thinking of their lost youth and the love which eluded them. Connie finishes her aria with a smile and a tear, then hastens from the dais to link arms with her waiting lover. And that heart-throbbing climax in 'First Love' was more than worthy of repetition in a subsequent film, 'His Butler's Sister' where, although the setting was more spectacular, the circumstances were not dissimilar.

Though one might have expected any variation of the Cinderella theme to portray in some measure the eternal conflict between good and evil, 'First Love' did not deal portentously with that conflict in respect of its two principal characters. But it provided a fascinating contrast between the dark and imperious Barbara (in an ugly sister role) and the self-effacing Connie whose lovely face seemed to reflect the humility and tenderness softening her approach to life and to society at large. Barbara, whose philosophy was wholly hedonistic, did not think of her beautiful cousin as a dear little girl with endearing ways, but rather an encumbrance in her home. As such she would ensure that Connie had a very limited social agenda. If she (Barbara) had her way, and no course more vindictive, all such social activity would be curtailed to the point when Connie's status might be regarded as no more than that of a servant in the household. She saw not deference but timidity in Connie's earnest desire to fit in amicably with her new family and especially never to disturb her uncle, a whimsical character who cherished peace and quiet in his own little sanctuary, secure from a cackling wife with her head in astrological clouds, a pretty but egotistical daughter and a son whose complacency and indolence was beyond belief. It was well perhaps that, as she said in the film, Deanna had made up her mind to 'like everybody and to make everybody like me'. And I can only comment that if she had employed the second 'like' otherwise than in a transitive sense grammatically, the difficulty of conversion might have made the task a Herculean one, indeed one for the Creator alone and not a girl who was as gentle as she was ingenuous.

I must confess that in my view it would be churlish of anyone, professional analyst or amateur critic like myself, to look for shortcomings in the plot or characterisation of so absorbing and delightful a film as 'First Love' certainly was. Its script writers were excellent, its direction by the duo, Joe Pasternak and Henry Koster, masterly throughout. My own observations, I must admit, were not framed with the sort of objectivity which might be expected of an established critic. All I sought to do was to convey my impression of sequences in the film which illustrated in a definitive way Deanna's unique talents as an actress and singer – the little mannerisms such as 'toying with her fingers' while feeling lost without a partner in a vast ballroom – her deprecatory smile and furrowed brow when she thought the master of ceremonies was referring to herself when in a fulsome introduction he spoke of 'a very shy young lady with the gift of song', of an 'inspired talent' and 'charming personality' whom he hoped to persuade to sing. Who, witness to her eventual genial self-assurance – the little snap of the finger when she chided a confused compere who was groping for her name and kept getting it wrong – would have felt the slightest sympathy for an indignant, middle-aged, overweight prima donna whom she had unwittingly unstaged?

'First Love' was not intended to be a vehicle for drama or tragicomedy on the classic scale nor to subscribe to the formula, now I hope discredited, of eschewing happy endings – the syndrome of misery exemplified by Romeo and Juliet which in its particular field is the apotheosis for literary gloom-mongers and disciples of Melpomine. On the contrary it is a prescription for laughter and for the tears which are but overtones of joy; it is a festival of flowers which, as Deanna puts it so musically, 'in bloom, banish the gloom.' It is purely and simply a fairy-tale and with Deanna in the title role it was infused with the gladness and romance which all normal humans crave. Only a heart crippled by prejudice could fail to respond to its rhythms and rejoicings. Deanna's shy hesitancy when she received her first screen kiss, her sweet abstraction immediately afterwards – the wide-eyed, unblinking gaze and innocent wonderment which punctuated her performance – above all the divine resonance of her singing voice – these are the positive elements which make 'First Love' a masterpiece of a special kind. And that is the kind which gives unqualified pleasure, a balm to the doleful mind and lights the torch of fantasy to brighten a mundane world. Yet as the film unfolded, few exaggerations were discernible. It was a fairy-tale but not improbable in that respect. No time for gloomy introspection while watching it. It was and is an antidote to pessimism and Deanna is the goddess supreme above all.

Chapter 8

It's a Date

The heyday of the Hollywood film industry, the Thirties and Forties, produced a plethora of talent for world viewing. A procession of actors and actresses who have come to be regarded as giants of the cinematic art paraded across the silver screen – some in respect of their special roles of hero or villain, dashing romanticist or contemptible rake, saint or psychopath, were celebrities whose names are not easily forgotten, in particular perhaps those who were associated with the sagas of the American legendary Wild West. Hollywood, where moguls of the film world presided in exclusive state, was the undoubted capital of the kingdom which fostered the proliferation of a form of entertainment unchallenged by the theatre or a television project still in the development stage. With the need for success at the box office the primary religion, Hollywood was nothing if not consistent and well-tried formulas were repeated *ad nauseum*. Perhaps it was not simply fortuitous then that in the characters she was called upon to play Deanna Durbin was singularly unfortunate in the matter of parentage. In her early films a sweet, little soul was never accorded the privilege of enjoying a normal, fulfilling home life with a doting mother and father to shield her from life's attritions. In 'Three Smart Girls" her parents were estranged, in 'One Hundred Men and a Girl' we see her as the fifteen-year-old daughter of a widower valiantly keeping house for him, in 'Mad About Music' the reverse situation applies – she has a mother widowed at an early age, and in 'First Love' she plays the part of an orphan. We begin to wonder what worse calamity can befall her than having no parents at all when, lo and behold, the producers have relented, though not entirely, because a poor lady's husband is deceased like the one in 'Mad About Music'. And very inconveniently for the young widow in Deanna's film 'It's a Date' he has died leaving her with a baby girl scarcely out of the cradle.

In view of these repeated defections by one or other or both of her elders, it would not have been surprising had Deanna reacted with a certain sangfroid instead of the quiet resignation which marked her acceptance of such situations.

In 'It's a Date' Deanna finds herself once again the daughter of a widow whose career lies in the world of entertainment save that in this instance the talented mother is a star of the live theatre and not the cinema. Deanna appears under the name of Pamela Drake, a young and aspiring actress who worships her mother and hopes to emulate her in achieving success in the theatre. While her mother goes on holiday to Honolulu, taking with her the script of a new production in which she will play a major role, Pamela is auditioned by the producer and the author of the play who are really looking for someone much younger than Pamela's mother to star in it. The audition takes place on a student campus and the two magnates of the theatre seize the opportunity of assessing the merits of their forthcoming drama by permitting a group of student actors and actresses to make up the entire cast. Pamela gives such an assured performance in the lead role, her singing of 'Loch Lomond' is so exquisite, that they decide immediately to give her her chance in the grand venue of New York's theatreland. She is overjoyed at her sudden good fortune, but thinking that her experienced mother might give her help and advice, she

decides to travel to Honolulu, studying her script on the voyage. There
follows a delightful interlude on shipboard when a millionaire who has
made his fortune in the growing and distribution of pineapples and
happens to be on his way home from the mainland to his home in
Hawaii pretends to be a stowaway to test Pamela's reaction to his
plight. Covertly he has watched her talking to herself (as he imagines)
in a distressful way when she has simply been rehearsing her lines,
and he assumes that she is burdened with grief or a misfortune of
some kind. But he is convinced that she has a compassionate spirit and
has a bet with the ship's captain, an old friend, that she will respond to
his overtures. He is not disappointed in that assumption but his plan
backfires when he finds himself having to remain for long periods in a
cramped lifeboat while Pamela plies him to bursting-point with food
obtained from a co-operative steward. She is so deceived by his play-
acting and so absorbed in her guise of good Samaritan that when she
thinks his presence is about to be discovered by a search party
organised for fun by the captain she creates a diversion by jumping
overboard. Of course, a chivalrous millionaire, amazed at the lengths
she will go to protect him, leaps to her rescue. Both have a thorough
ducking before they are pulled on board, at which point Pamela
discovers that she has been the victim of a hoax. She is not easily
mollified but eventually all is put right by the millionaire's whimsical
manner and sense of humour. Pamela succumbs to his charm and even
imagines that he has fallen in love with her. Ashore she is in for
another surprise when she finds her mother immersed in the very role
for which she has already been chosen. Then the millionaire pineapple
farmer meets mother and there is love at first sight between them. So
Pamela's mother accepts his offer of marriage and turns her back on
the theatre to share domestic bliss with the one whom poor Pamela
thought was going to propose to herself. There is both humour and
irony in mother's suggestion that her daughter would be ideal for the
role she has decided to abandon. Pamela, after denouncing men as
deceivers ever, is left with a clear path to Broadway and unstinted
applause at an exciting and triumphant debut.

From the arrival of Pamela in Honolulu until her transfer to the glamour of the New York theatre, there is a wealth of funny and intriguing situations depicting many a romantic rendezvous – lavish party scenes with the elite of an island society at play and the decor of grand ballrooms, always brilliant with magnificent chandeliers and cascading lights. On then to the film's heart-warming climax with Pamela's rendering of 'Ave Maria' in a crowded hall. She is Madonna-like as she sings in a cloistered sanctuary – a calm, unruffled figure – a perfect dream of beauty and of grace. She is breathtakingly visual and your soul takes wing with her song.

Although 'It's a Date' was not screened until after the premiere of 'First Love' in which Deanna first became involved in an affair of the heart (despite her youth and innocence, or it may be because of them) she reverts to playing the role of a girl who is still young enough for her feelings for a man much older than herself to be regarded, by her mother at least, as childish infatuation, an obsession more markedly evident in 'That Certain Age'. And though Deanna acts maturely there are still strong nuances of tender girlhood about her in this later film, albeit there is no crowd of importunate teenagers milling about her to remind her of her youth and inexperience.

Her partner in a delightful escapade, Walter Pidgeon, is a much more sympathetic character in a difficult part than was Melvyn Douglas in a comparable situation in 'That Certain Age'. That is a personal view, however. Pidgeon shows no trace of cynicism in his association with a young and impressionable actress who has conceived a liking for him, or something even more fond, and he is at pains to disillusion her without giving affront or chafing her sensitivities too severely. That ultimately her pride is not too seriously wounded by his rejection of her in favour of her mother becomes apparent in the penultimate sequence of the film when she grapples with the knowledge that she is unwanted, in a very demonstrative fashion. Her mother, her former reluctant suitor and moguls of the theatre are treated to a rhetoric which is drawn verbatim from the theatrical production in which she is due to star. Her 'I'm through with men' may not be the classic riposte of all time from a girl facing up to the reality of unrequited love but it is fair to say that in a moment of high drama Deanna gave the phrase such an expression of finality as to leave no doubt whatever of her belief in the duplicity and worthlessness of the male.

'It's a Date' is memorable above all, as one would expect of a Deanna Durbin movie, for its beautiful melodies and the star's inspired singing. At a party in Honolulu where a dyed-in-the-wool bachelor at last succumbs to feminine lure in an unexpected way as regards his final choice of lifelong partner, Deanna gives a thrilled audience Musetta's Waltz Song from 'La Bohème' and receives a rapturous ovation. Equally enthralling is her rendition of Schubert's 'Ave Maria' in the closing act of St. Joan. The camera gives a close-up of Deanna in monastic robes, and her face is so angelic, so utterly composed, as to make the most dispassionate of humans catch their breath or find themselves bereft of all volition. She looks so unutterably at peace with the world, with all Creation, that you can but feel in her expression the true essence of divinity, something perfect and undefiled. Her person and her devotional hymn more faithfully mirror the sanctity which is erroneously applied to the musty crypt, the austere cell and the dark corridors of the nunnery. I cannot believe that any voice has ever sung, or ever will sing, the holy salutation of 'Ave Maria' with the thrilling quality of tone which came so naturally to Deanna. In the same context I must pay tribute to her singing of 'Loch Lomond' in an earlier scene in the film. I have heard that immortal ballad sung a thousand times or more during my lifetime by all manner of vocalists. I have heard it sung sensibly and competently in a traditional way, enlivened by instrumentalists, even jazzed up by artists, who, if I may so describe them, are specialists in mediocrity. Nor do I doubt that it has been further degraded by other crude interpreters of music. But Deanna's version invests it with a haunting mystery and spirituality that makes one forget a sorrowful theme and a sad farewell and remember only the melody itself. For it is an ethereal song as Deanna sings it, with sounds which are exquisite to the ear, reaching to perfection in the vocal art.

Although 'It's a Date' is an unforgettable odyssey of laughter and wit, of the human spirit in many manifestations bubbling like champagne – and delightful venues, always decorative, sometimes exotic, where indulgence and enjoyment are not marred by spurious pretension or conversation by false conceits and suspicion of elitism. Deanna in cocktail dress or informal wear is always captivating, whatever her mood. One feels – I always do – that any sophistication in her acting is purely involuntary, that she is still the adorable little creature we came to love and admire in 'Three Smart Girls'. Here is no synthetic charm but the emanation of a wonderful personality.

Chapter 9

Spring Parade

Deanna's eighth film, 'Spring Parade', reached the cinema soon after the German blitzkrieg of 1940 and its theme was in sharp contrast with the dolorous nature of life outside the haven of the cinema. It reminded me instantly of the fairy stories and fables which, like the nameless host of my contemporaries similarly disposed, I read so avidly when I was young, but not so young as not to harbour premonitions about romance and the pursuit of love. I read of misty empires, of lost lands which flourished in the deeps of time past, of pomp and pageantry, of kings and princes and the hapless peasantry which sustained a privileged elite in its extravagance and glory. And so when first I saw 'Spring Parade' and its opening sequence of a peasant girl leading a refractory goat to market against a background of dark forests and snowy mountains, my thoughts flashed back to those halcyon days of the past when my spirit often journeyed afar to mysterious lands; when giants, witches and wizards and invincible warriors wielding might broadswords were far from mythical figures in my lively imagination. They were not improbable beings in a juvenile mind – in fact the chimera of Antiquity found safe lodging there until I became more conscious of the true realities of mortal existence, so many austere and stern, and the inescapable monotony of a mundane environment. So any form of escapism, especially that which resuscitated the illusions and fond yearnings of long-vanished years, was a diversion to be welcomed and cherished with the whole heart thereafter as a counter to cynicism and disbelief. I found in 'Spring Parade' and its extravaganza of song and dance, like music in delirium, that precise diversion. That diversion is now a journey a half-century back in time to the previous springtime of memory. The halcyon days were the genesis of that memory.

What a light-hearted romp 'Spring Parade' was! Though I have no means of knowing whether the producer of that film kept faithful to the original story by Ernst Marischka, the end result was more than simply pleasurable. If there was fantasy – and there was – it was the implausibility of a peasant girl from a remote mountain village in an old-time Austria, withal one with a voice of operatic quality, meeting in mutual accord (including a very plebeian smack of the hand to seal a bargain – and that, mark you, without a sign of royal condescension) with an emperor and his glittering entourage. Yet I suppose that strange improbability which is the secret of the true fairy-tale, added to the charm of the illusion. Literally, every step of the way to the imperial presence since the peasant girl who is known by the rather uninspiring name of Ilonka is first heard singing 'It's Foolish But It's Fun' as she strides blithely forward to sell her goat, is an incident to beguile the spirit and induce laughter. Especially mirth-provoking was Mischa Auer's frantic dancing in his efforts to acquire a goat without having to pay for it (and incidentally I feared for Deanna when she was thrown bodily across the dance arena) – a triumphant but exhausted Ilonka falling asleep on a baker's cart loaded with straw and being transported unwittingly to Vienna – and the peasant girl, safely ensconced at last in a baker's household where she has been given temporary lodging, shedding innumerable petticoats in an hilarious bedroom scene. As she stepped out of them I believe I counted eleven. It must have been devilishly cold among the mountains where Ilonka lived.

Other scenes there were, some joyous, some full of a dreamy tranquillity, as touching as they were entertaining. Ever memorable is Ilonka's doe-eyed admiration and speculative wonder as she looks down smiling from a casement upon a parade of jolly bandsmen in the street below – and the 'waltzing high on a cloud' episode in an Austrian beer-garden. In this sequence comes an intermission when Ilonka is temporarily disengaged from her partner's embrace while they are dancing. Her happiness is such that for a moment she forgets she is in Vienna and adopts a posture with hand on hip more suited to her native village than a sophisticated, urban night-spot. Swiftly, however, she realises that Viennese etiquette is markedly different to that in a rural backwater. Much less mindful of a cultural gulf is she when she haggles with an astonished proprietor over the price of a meal.

A simple and uncomplicated plot deals with the varying fortunes of an Austrian peasant-girl who, belying her humble background, migrates to the illustrious court of an emperor. There she meets with love in the person of an army corporal who in addition to his talents as a musician has ability as a composer. Their enchantment with each other, fostered as much by her singing as the exuberant quality of his tunes and librettos, is dimmed only temporarily when, seeing her dining with a gentleman who has the ear of the emperor, he becomes insanely jealous and is rude to her. But he is unaware that Ilonka is simply trying to persuade an influential companion to intercede with the emperor on behalf of her friendly host, the baker, who has wrongly been committed to prison. Ilonka succeeds in getting the baker released and appointed as supplier to the emperor's court. The corporal, thanks to a letter written by Ilonka, is detailed to conduct the imperial orchestra while the girl herself is invited to the palace for a rendition with that marvellous singing voice of hers. Though aggrieved at first by having to stand close to a youthful conductor whom she has not yet forgiven for his rudeness at their last meeting, Ilonka starts to sing. Ironically it is only when inadvertently he raps her over the head with his baton that she realises that a fortune-teller at the fair was true in his prediction that she would marry an artist in Vienna, love coming her way at last with the help of a big stick. And so to the spectacular ending of the film in the vast ballroom of the royal palace with Ilonka and her lover, now reconciled, whirling across the floor to the tune of 'Waltzing High on a Cloud'.

'Spring Parade' is a grand festival of fun and glorious melody and Deanna in the person of Ilonka a perfect dream of delight.

Chapter 10

Nice Girl?

D eanna Durbin's next film 'Nice Girl?' was presumably intended to give her admirers a mild shock, with a question mark giving a vague hint of impropriety. Once again as in 'That Certain Age' and 'It's a Date' Deanna is called upon to play the role of a girl still in the transitional stage from adolescence to young womanhood. She is attracted to the roving representative of a scientific organisation, one who is handsome and personable and not unromantic, but one whom traditionalists in the area of love and marriage might well consider far too mature for a girl as inexperienced and innocent as Deanna. She gives an assured and convincing performance with the right touch of hesitancy and guarded awareness of the predatory male which often lurks beneath the cultured exterior. She lives in a provincial American township where she is generally regarded as a 'nice girl', this time without any qualifications as regards punctuation. And in this respect she differs from her two sisters whose reputation, because of their rather flirtatious disposition, is not deemed so immaculate. Her boy friend whom she has known since their schooldays is more interested in motor cars than romance – at least he gives that impression because he is never very explicit about his true feelings where his heart is concerned, as distinct from his ambition in respect of his career as a mechanic and engineer of remarkable ability. He builds his own car which incorporates enough technical refinements to bewilder even experts in automobile technology and terrify novices in that field. The consequence becomes clear when the agent from the scientific foundation must return to New York after the completion of his business with Deanna's father. Still in close pursuit of romance, Deanna has volunteered to drive him to the local railway station. Her plan is that he should miss his train, in which eventuality she will suggest that he travel to New York by car instead. She of course will be the chauffeur. For her strategy to succeed she must somehow reduce the car's speed to a snail's pace and does so by stuffing a potato into the rear exhaust pipe of her boy friend's 'wonder' car which he has generously placed at her disposal. Incidentally she is also indebted to her boy friend for the little trick with the potato, a ruse which he has demonstrated during the course of tuition which he has been giving her out of sheer enthusiasm. Poor soul, he never dreamed that his wily girl friend might make use of such knowledge. The scientist of course misses his train as the girl intended, but a bystander draws his attention to the obstruction in the exhaust pipe and he is much amused and intrigued by a stratagem which Jane (Deanna's name in this little adventure) attributes to her younger and mischievous sister. Jane shrugs off any embarrassment and she drives thereafter to New York in a much more normal fashion. Unfortunately, when a rainstorm develops and the car-hood fails to function properly (because of a flawed mechanical genius perhaps) they are both soaked to the skin and arrive in a sorry state at the scientist's New York address. The romantic developments in a well-appointed mansion is light comedy at its best. Jane bathes and dons a fetching pyjama suit and looks the picture of elegance as she toys with a champagne glass on an executive's bed. A butler, looking bland but very discreet after Jane has agreed to stay the night with his employer, holds up her wet clothes and says that they will be dried and laundered by the morning. When the door closes on a smiling butler a slightly apprehensive Jane scans the face of her host (played by the incorrigible Lothario, Franchot Tone) and begins to wonder whether her seduction during the coming night is more than a possibility. On the contrary his part demands that he should be mindful that his lovely guest is the daughter of a colleague; and though he is very taken with her, he is too much of a gentleman to make any improper advances. Then the telephone rings and she hears him conversing with his mother. He makes a joke of the day's events and the drama of the potato. His meaning is clear – a rather foolish and romantic young girl has designs upon him. Jane is resentful, upbraids him spiritedly and when he retires for the night to his own den she flees the mansion. She has no alternative save to undertake the long drive home in her pyjama outfit. And oh! the confusion and the atmosphere of scandal in the early morning when she reaches the vicinity of her provincial home and the horn of her boy friend's car starts blaring like a klaxon. She lacks the know-how to stop the noise. With dogs barking frenziedly, neighbours yelling from open windows for quiet, a distracted Jane abandons the vehicle and dashes for home. She races upstairs to bed, locking her door upon a world which suddenly seems to have become insane. Naturally, in view of the unwonted hour of her homecoming and the nature of her attire, everyone including her own household is convinced that she has not spent the night with a man in New York discussing the breeding cycle of rabbits, notwithstanding that her father, an expert on heredity, keeps such creatures for experimental purposes. She learns later that only her trusting boy friend believes that she has returned undefiled from a brief escapade, and is not altogether pleased to be taken for granted.

As might be anticipated, Jane survives a droll experience which her understanding father describes as 'a five cent scandal', an apologetic executive hurrying back from New York, supports her loyally in a prospective marriage farce to disarm her critics (not without seizing the opportunity of kissing her passionately more than once) and eventually Jane is reconciled with the young man who has never wavered in his allegiance.

In 'Nice Girl?' Deanna's singing is more blissful than ebullient save perhaps the final song before the curtain comes down, i.e. 'Thank You America'. That is a stirring and rollicking anthem, by no means jingoistic in its patriotic summons to America's youth, and Deanna sings it with an engaging and merry lilt. The camera swings over a crowded parade-ground with every face turned towards a military band and a dais where Deanna is a striking figure of serene charm and bewitching femininity. Pride, even exaltation, is everywhere manifest in the martial mien and not least the captivation that all men present without exception feel for a beautiful and talented girl who, apart from her natural appeal, is a symbol of the beloved land and its ancient institutions they are gathering to protect. In this film there are no operatic arias but dreamy songs like 'Beneath the Lights of Home', 'Old Folks at Home' (which surely could not offend even the racial and 'politically correct' fanatics who infest the world today), 'Love at Last', sung so beguilingly in a bachelor's apartment, and lastly that delightful lyric 'Perhaps'. The rendition is given almost casually in the opening shots of the film while her approving father listens covertly. The venue is a cellar improvised as a rabbitry by Jane's father who is an experimental scientist. I daresay Deanna's song was a pleasant stimulus to the procreative urges of the lucky inmates (the quadrupeds of course).

'Nice girl?' is but another diverting fairy-tale in a modern setting. All it lacked for me was an aria or two from the works of the great composers of the past. When one recalls Deanna's 'Nessun Dorma' in 'His Butler's Sister' one can only regret that similar scope was not accorded a glorious voice in Deanna's ninth film. In all other respects this film splendidly illustrated Deanna's talent as an actress of the greatest competence and sensitivity.

Chapter 11

——— ⌁ ———

It Started with Eve

'It Started With Eve', Deanna's next film, is a superb, romantic comedy, albeit one with an amorphous title. And I shall take the liberty of examining it in detail since I consider it the best film Deanna ever made, with 'His Butler's Sister' a close second. The characterisation achieved by Charles Laughton in his first partnership with Deanna is brilliant but in her own unpretentious way she herself gives an outstanding performance which is not overshadowed by her famous co-star. Mind you, there are not the usual demands on a glorious voice, which is a pity, but the occasions when she *does* sing are more than memorable. I would have preferred it, however, if Deanna had been allowed to complete her repertoire without interruption – in other words, to a satisfying finish. The waltz from the Sleeping Beauty ballet by Tchaikovsky was suspended before reaching its climax, as was 'Going Home' towards the end of the film when Deanna and Laughton were in the midst of a poignant scene of mingled reunion and farewell. I remember a very touching moment in 'First Love' when Deanna was singing 'Home Sweet Home' and was similarly overcome by emotion so that she was unable to finish her song. Perhaps that instance in 'It Started With Eve' was the most distressful. Laughton's 'I'm terribly fond of you, you know – terribly fond' – and Deanna's tearful, throbbing solo 'I'm a goin' home – 'It's not far', etcetera, infused their performance with an extraordinary pathos. In Deanna's case hers was the heartbreak of loving someone who was seemingly indifferent and pledged to another.

In marked contrast with the haunting sadness of 'Goin' Home', Deanna sings something earlier in the film which she calls 'a little Spanish number, 'Clavelitos'. The first time I heard it I marvelled that any vocalist should be capable of such swift intonation and a clear enunciation of the words of a lively and stimulating song. As she sang the melody accelerated, as it were, the tune was engaging, the rhythm electric but serene and the words themselves seemed to be dancing their own jig upon her tongue. Clavelitos is the sort of challenge which only a supreme artist could meet with the kind of equanimity which characterised Deanna's performance.

Here I must mention that I have watched 'It Started with Eve' so many times that I can quote verbatim much of the dialogue with ease. And therefore I can say with assurance that there are so many comments, remarks, interjections and asides in this film which, if not veritable witticisms, give rise to a broad grin or impulsive laughter. Deserving of mention, Wade Boteler, who played various small parts in Deanna Durbin films, is really priceless in the opening sequence. He is a newspaper editor momentarily expecting to learn of the death of a millionaire tycoon who is dangerously ill. He has already prepared the front page of an edition announcing the expected demise and the necessary obituary. So anxious is he that a life should be terminated (because he considers it a foregone conclusion anyway) that he declares to a rival in the newspaper industry that 'he [Jonathan Reynolds, the rich businessman seemingly doomed] is going to die for me, not the Herald', and he adopts a prayerful attitude as if addressing the Almighty, saying, 'Please, if he must go, let him go by 9.20', presumably the deadline for publication of the evening edition. Strangely enough the wish does not sound in any way macabre or unfeeling, it just strikes one as being not merely droll, but irresistibly funny. Boteler achieves the same effect shortly afterwards in a telephone conversation with a hapless reporter detailed to keep a close eye on the Reynolds mansion and to advise his office of a celebrity's passing. His parting shot to the reporter is 'Frank, I'm warning you, if Reynolds isn't dead within the next half-hour, don't come back here.'

The plot starts to unfold in real earnest with Reynolds' son arriving home from a holiday in Mexico accompanied by his fiancée, Gloria Pennington, and her unprepossessing mother who, when agitated, has a habit of twirling a string of beads with the most steely glint conceivable in her beady eye. Junior leaves them at an hotel and hurries to his father's bedside. Presumably Jonathan has been informed by letter of his son's latest romance for, still lucid despite his illness, he asks to see the girl whom his son intends to marry. When Reynolds junior dashes to the hotel where Gloria and her mother are staying he finds they have left on a shopping expedition and is completely distracted because he believes his father's death is imminent and he is anxious to satisfy a dying man's wish. And it is at this point that Deanna is introduced into the film. She has the name of Anne Terry and is a cloakroom attendant in the reception hall of the hotel (though this is but a stop-gap job for an aspiring singer from Ohio who for two years or more has been seeking sponsorship in the operatic world and spending most of her earnings on voice training).

We meet her as she takes a ticket from an obviously wealthy financier who is collecting his overcoat at the desk in the foyer. Chatting with a colleague he makes a casual reference to a 'paltry' sum of 25,000 dollars for standing in for a director at his office for two weeks. Anne is given a tip from that unlovable twain which she holds up at arms' length for inspection, remarking, 'This must be the new five-dollar coin they're putting out.' Then she flips the coin idly, adding 'Looks like the same old dime to me. They're diming us to death.'

A whimsical touch this and one of many instances of slick humour in a film which seldom calls for gravity or serious contemplation.

Anne's shift that day comes to an end and as she leaves the hotel for her lodgings her departure coincides with Jonathan junior's sudden inspiration of finding a temporary substitute for Gloria Pennington, his fiancée. After all he tells himself, if his father is about to die, he would wish him to die happy, and deceit in a good cause would be forgivable anyway. And it is thus that Anne feels herself seized upon outside the foyer of the hotel by a young man in a highly agitated and emotional state who gabbles something about a ' dying father – 'Please, I'll give you fifty dollars.'

My own view is that most girls would have regarded such an outburst as the bizarre ruse of a man with sinister designs on female virtue and called instantly for help from any passer-by. But the rain is torrential and the rush of traffic confusing, and Anne, bewildered, absently trying to fold her umbrella, is bundled into a taxi where her abductor gives a more coherent explanation of his behaviour and persuades his 'pick-up' to pose as his fiancée so that a dying man might close his eyes in peace in the belief that his son had at last found the girl of his dreams.

That wondering face, illumined by a table lamp strategically placed to give a perfect perspective of its lovely contours, draws his gaze and after a moment or two he smiles and mumbles 'Pretty'. He bids her to sit on his bed and takes her hand in his own tender clasp. He continues talking in a sentimental tone and between pauses watches closely the young woman decorously seated close beside him. He uses such phrases as 'We've had some lovely women in *our* family. You should have seen his mother. You'll fit in just fine. My, you're pretty.' Later, he adds, 'I've had a good life – I never missed anything.' Anne is deeply moved and sobs slightly. The old man seems suddenly to tire, blinks and turns his head aside as though intimating that he is ready to depart on his last, long journey.

This unusual experience for a provincial lass, unused to an ambience of wealth and luxury which lesser mortals (strictly in a material sense) only dream about, is an augury of future complications in the life of Reynolds junior if, as seems decidedly probable, his father survives. Anne is almost apologetic that evening when she accepts the promised fifty dollars for playing the part of a promised bride. Out she goes in the rain, then, poor child, ready to use the money for train fare back to a life of obscurity in a remote little township in Ohio.

But the next morning with his son and his doctor (whom he regards as an irritating quack) sitting silently in his bedchamber and momentarily expecting to hear the final spasms of a very sick man, while down in the main hall two lugubrious artisans from a local museum wait to take his death-mask, the elder Reynolds comes wide awake and declares abruptly, 'I'm hungry – I want my breakfast.' The doctor instantly summons an attendant nurse and instructs her to prepare a thin slice of toast soaked in warm milk, whereat Jonathan senior asks reprovingly, 'Are you feeding the cat in here? I want a steak and a cigar.' Nurse intervenes – I'll get you some nice, warm toasty," and Jonathan's indignant retort is, 'I want some nice, warm steaky.' Next he turns to his son and expresses his wish to see 'Gloria', naturally unaware that Anne has been a substitute for the real Gloria Pennington. As might well be imagined, Junior's consternation is acute and he tries to make excuses until his irate parent bawls, 'For heaven's sake go and get her!'

Fortunately Junior remembers the name of the little town in Ohio whither Anne is bound by early train that morning and he dashes off to the railway station to arrive just in time to stop Anne climbing aboard her train. So follows another amusing scene with Reynolds junior prattling about his father's wish to see his son's fiancée once more and afraid that if it is not gratified he will have a further relapse, while two of Anne's friends who have accompanied her to the station to bid farewell look on in amazement. One is an elderly woman who, seeing Anne literally bundled away with her baggage, asks what all the fuss is about. The younger female, a girl who has shared Anne's lodgings in New York, replies, 'Don't worry – it's platonic – he wants her for his father!' That line is an excellent example of Hollywood humour at its best.

When Anne for the second time enters Jonathan's bedroom, having been warned not to say anything which might disclose her false identity, two visitors, the local bishop and a curate, enthuse over her charm and good looks. The bishop has been told that the fiancée comes from Mexico and having some command of the native tongue himself makes one or two observations in that language. But Anne smiles without hesitation and moving gracefully around the bed says in a cautionary tone, 'Now, bishop'. She makes it appear that what the bishop has said is a trifle indiscreet and that she would deprecate any further discussion of the subject.

At Jonathan's request Anne then opens a safe in the adjacent wall and takes forth a black box containing the family jewels. While his son views the proceedings in great agitation, Jonathan tells her that a very valuable and wonderfully fashioned necklace which she removes from the casket on his instructions is hers to keep and to pass on in her turn within the family. I particularly relished his rebuke to his son when that rather crass individual, dismayed because his father has revealed the combination of the safe, tries to snatch the jewels away. 'Are you planning to wear them yourself?' says he.

When Junior leaves the room to escort the bishop and his aide downstairs, Anne and the irrepressible character in the bed exchange confidences and there follows a hilarious scene in which the patient smokes one of his very expensive but favourite cigars and Anne counts the puffs, imposing a limit of ten puffs which has not been reached when the doctor who has been examining Jonathan's mail returns unexpectedly. Jonathan surreptitiously whips the hand holding the cigar under the bedclothes, but the doctor, sniffing the air suspiciously, sees smoke filtering from the bottom of the bed. He confiscates not only the offending cigar but a whole box in a bedside cabinet. Then he looks reprovingly at Anne who replies archly to a grumbling medic – 'Don't look at me – I smoke a pipe.' A lovely aside that from a guileless girl. Later when Anne proposes to sing for him, Jonathan, who knows nothing about her vocal abilities, is quite adamant that he is in no condition to listen, but both he and the doctor are willing converts to her delightful whims when they hear her glorious tones ringing through the mansion. Displaying all the vitality of youth in her supple movements, Anne has tripped swiftly down to the vast hall below and with the help of two 'death-mask operatives' pushed a grand piano into position at the foot of an imposing stairway.

Deanna Durbin in 'It Started with Eve'.
(Reproduced courtesy of The Movie Store Collection)

She calls up the stair to Jonathan, 'Can you hear me?' The reply comes back – a thunderous 'No'. She pounds the keys and repeats the question, whereat he yells – 'Go on, break every chandelier in the house!'

Drowsing spectres in that venerable, old building awaken to the entrancing melody of 'When I sing the cares of the day are far away', followed by 'When I sing the world is a place that's bright and gay', and an invisible cataract of the sweetest sound that was ever unleashed in that carved dwelling sweeps between fluted column and entablature, trailing echoes in its wake. And so Anne sings to the strains of the dreamlike waltz from 'The Sleeping Beauty' ballet by Tchaikovsky while her supple fingers dance on the piano keys in a perfect accompaniment. Forth from the sickroom comes the doctor full of approbation, to lean on the balustrade on a galleried landing and enjoy an impromptu concert. And on his feet for the first time after a lengthy illness, though still unsteady, Jonathan moves from his bed to the floor giving on to the stairway. He looks an incongruous figure as he totters forward and a trifle pathetic in his long night-shirt. Anne is startled at his sudden appearance but is reassured when she detects his warm smile and her lips curve in delicious response as effortlessly she continues to sing. No strain whatever as the highest notes come rippling forth. Jonathan is enraptured by the lively and heart-searing bliss of a renewed burst of song and there cannot be a doubt that a recovery, sparked in his darkest hour by a lovely and compassionate young woman tearful at his bedside, will benefit still further from Anne's musical therapy.

The film never loses its initial momentum – clever dialogue – unexpected twists in the plot – droll mannerisms – sometimes merely humorous, often funny and evoking spontaneous laughter.

As a consequence of Anne's improvised concert in his mansion an enthusiastic millionaire decides to throw a party for her so that influential people, including perhaps Leopold Stokowsky, the famous conductor, can hear her sing and appreciate her potential as an opera star or perhaps in some other niche in the world of musical entertainment. But Jonathan junior, still seemingly unaware how vastly more attractive and desirable his 'bogus fiancée' is than the real Gloria Pennington, has other ideas. At the first opportunity he informs his father that there has been a quarrel between himself and Anne, that she has a fiery temper and even struck him over the head with her handbag – all of which was a prelude to breaking off their engagement. Jonathan senior is shocked, saying he thought the girl was 'so mild and gentle'. After reflection he declares 'She liked me'. His son thereupon adds weight to his accusation about Anne by telling his father that she called the father a 'pompous, overbearing imitation of a dictator'.

Just at that moment the butler opens the hall door to admit Anne whose arrival is quite unexpected. She sheds her coat and comes running swiftly, albeit with appealing grace, to nestle her head against

Junior's chest and holding him close in her arms. Tearfully apologetic, she cries 'Forgive me, Johnny – please say you forgive me – I'm such a silly girl – It's my terrible temper.' Johnny's impulse is to expose the whole masquerade from the beginning whereat her lamentations become shrill in order to drown his words before any revelation reaches Jonathan's ear. The old man becomes angry with his son and bellows, 'For heaven's sake say you forgive her!'

When the trio calm down Johnny strides to a settee and sits down at a loss what to do next while mischievous old Jonathan nudges Anne and urges her to 'make it up'. He smiles and says, knowingly, 'That's why lovers quarrel, isn't it?'

Hesitantly Anne approaches Johnny and as she bends forward demurely to plant a decorous kiss upon his cheek he seizes her, pulls her across his lap and kisses her fervently as might a lover who is consumed with passion. As Anne struggles in his arms, mewing with desperation, he keeps his lips compressed to her own by sheer brute force, as it were.

Now I always thought that there was a code dictated by the Hollywood hierarchy that a screen kiss had to be of limited duration – seven or eight seconds approximately. It was my distinct impression that in 'It Started with Eve' Robert Cummings as Jonathan junior came near to breaching this particular directive when with Deanna imprisoned in his grasp he kissed her with undisguised passion, simulated or not. For once we see Deanna in a very sensual situation although I am sure she was not being deliberately provocative.

When at last Anne manages to come up for air he starts to tickle her in the ribs, perhaps in even tender places, until she becomes almost hysterical. But she retaliates spiritedly, tickling him in return and biting his ear as a chuckling Jonathan senior disappears behind one of the many pillars in a palatial house. When she finally breaks free there follows a frantic merry-go-round in the reception-hall with Anne expertly upending an armchair and striding over it till it reaches the horizontal plane. Johnny, however, lacks the expertise of his quarry and falls all over the place – frustrated, he retreats from the armchair in his path and tears back round a long, refectory-type table. At last, panting with exertion, both are obliged to pause in the chase, one at either end of the table. They argue loudly and old Jonathan hears their conversation from which he learns that Anne is not his son's real fiancée. Among the significant words Anne hurls at Johnny are – 'I told you I wanted to sing at the party. I'll tell your father the truth after Saturday night.'

The party in question is one which Jonathan has decided to arrange for Anne but the prospect of which induced Johnny to pretend that he had quarrelled with his fiancée. How could he permit Anne to be introduced as his future bride with the real Gloria waiting in the wings?

Jonathan is puzzled and dismayed by what he has overhead and thinks that a timely entrance is called for. He re-enters the room to find Anne seated at a piano and his son pretending all is well. Jonathan is so shocked that he hardly acknowledges Anne's query about the guest list for Saturday's party. But he nods affirmatively when she asks if he would like to hear her sing the number she has in mind for the occasion. Then this brief but extraordinarily tuneful song, 'Clavelitos', is performed by Anne with a lingual dexterity almost magical in its impact. Her lips pour forth a torrent of notes so swift in progression that they fall almost subliminally upon the ear. Jonathan looks stunned, as much by Anne's radiant smile as her singing and for the first time Johnny's face registers fascination, perhaps the dawning of love, as he realises that he is listening to a voice of remarkable quality. His pleasure is unfeigned. One can only guess what might have followed that joyous discovery but for an untimely interruption. His warm smile for Anne is replaced by an expression almost of consternation when his attention is diverted from the piano by the sight of two ladies, the daughter and her mother who accompanied him from Mexico, staring at him fixedly from the entrance-hall. Indeed, the mother's attitude, glaring at Anne, 'that girl' as she chooses to call her, for she has learned of Johnny's predicament, is one of undisguised hostility. This is far from diminished when Jonathan introduces Anne as his son's fiancée, Miss Gloria Pennington. She twirls a long string of beads viciously. Poor Anne – she is so plainly ill at ease, conscious of the deception she was forced into by chance more than intent, but she is mainly solicitous for old Jonathan who has become an unwitting accomplice in the conspiracy. When Junior has left the house to seek a reconciliation with Gloria, Anne resolves to make a full confession to Jonathan. She makes for his bedroom upstairs whither he has retired. One of the most touching scenes in the entire film is then enacted. Jonathan gently contrives to avoid Anne pouring out her heart to him, for he is well aware what is troubling her. He succeeds by pretending that despite his apparent recovery all is far from well with his health. He coughs, simulates choking as he goes through the motions of taking a pill which he has surreptitiously flung in the fire grate when Anne's back is turned. The pill conveniently explodes in the heat which provides Jonathan with another excuse for showing shock and distress. He looks altogether plaintive when he points to the bed and expresses the fear that he might end up there again. Tenderly he embraces the girl with a delicate restraint which is a masterly piece of acting. She 'hasn't the heart' as she later tells Johnny to 'tell him the truth', obviously fearful that by so doing she might worsen his condition.

Anne decides not to disrupt Johnny's life further and with his approval makes the excuse of a 'splitting headache' so as to avoid attending Jonathan's party for her. That brings yet another poignant moment in the film when over the telephone she tells Jonathan with raised voice, 'No, I don't want to see you. I don't want to see you ever again!'

Of course she is carried away by the emotion of having to be unkind to Jonathan in order to keep her promise to his son, as much as the bleak prospect of returning to Ohio and the obscurity of a provincial town. More than the pain of her secret love for Johnny, she is heartbroken at being obliged to forfeit the respect of an ageing man who has a deep respect for her and love in a paternal way.

Jonathan looks quite stunned when he puts down the telephone receiver, but he is shrewd enough to suspect that what he overheard when his son was chasing Anne at his home suggests that her cruel and dismissive words on the telephone should not be taken too seriously. With the connivance of his butler Jonathan escapes from the party and is directed to Anne's lodging by his chauffeur who is well aware of the girl's address. Anne is taken completely by surprise when he is admitted and her doleful looks reflect the deepest anguish when he says, 'So you never want to see me again?' Several other moving phrases escape his lips 'You were going to leave without saying goodbye?' – this time looking at her open suitcase and clothes ready for packing) and 'It's not a nice way for old friends to part – We are old friends, aren't we?'

Anne nods her head miserably and standing close to an old piano abstractedly begins to play the opening chords of 'Goin' Home'. 'Sing that for me,' says Jonathan promptly, and when she answers, 'I can't just now', he responds, 'Why, not even that? What have I done to you?'

Anne sits down and complies with his request, remembering his whispered words, 'I'm terribly fond of you, you know – terribly fond.' But she breaks down with a sob towards the end of the song. He pretends not to notice and inspects the evening gown she has set aside, the one she would have worn at the party but for the promise to Johnny not to attend in order not to complicate further his relationship with Gloria. Jonathan then suggests that he and Anne should spend the rest of the evening in a night club and say goodbye properly – somewhere, he adds, 'where nobody knows me'. 'Where nobody knows you?' repeats Anne, wide-eyed in her innocence and trust. She is thus inveigled to accompany an artful admirer to a night-spot in the locality. From the moment they enter a very pretentious clubroom Anne realises that her escort has, to use a colloquial phrase, 'pulled a fast one'. For the imperturbable Jonathan is greeted effusively from all sides by friends and acquaintances delighted to see him apparently restored to health and vigour.

Anne's beautifully manicured fingertips beat a tattoo on her tiny black evening bag as she pauses and regards him reprovingly while a waiter helps him divest himself of his overcoat. 'Nobody knows you, eh?' she admonishes and her expression is stern for once. But Jonathan is in no sense discomfited. He shows no sign of contrition as they are shown to a table overlooking the dance floor. And he has forgotten completely the half-chewed lamp chop which he has concealed in his breast pocket beside the handkerchief ruffled there. For at the party earlier the excellent array of meats on display at the table buffet had proved too much of a temptation to Jonathan and he had been nibbling a lamb chop when his doctor approached. Guessing what the doctor's reaction would be, Jonathan had hastily deposited the trophy in his breast pocket.

When Anne and Jonathan are seated, a scene follows which encapsulates to my mind some of the richest comedy that Hollywood ever screened in its grand and never-to-be-forgotten heyday. Humourless as well as lacking in compassion would be the one who could watch the sequence to which I refer without guffawing or perhaps wiping the tears of joy from his eyes. Laughton's millionaire is the marvellous eccentric as convincing in this episode as he was earlier in his supposed death-bed and Deanna as Anne gives an unblemished performance. When Anne sips a so called coconut drink which Jonathan has ordered and which he calls a Reynolds special, to determine whether there is any alcoholic content which might be injurious to his fragile health, its spirituous potency literally makes her gasp. She is instantly affected and grimaces in some confusion. Straightaway she relapses into tears which Jonathan realises do not relate entirely to the powerful intoxication of his drink. She looks so forlorn and wistful that Jonathan shrewdly declares, 'You *are* in love with my son, aren't you?' She does not dissent, and asks for a handkerchief to dry her tears. Still gazing upon her with a kind of paternal love and worship, Jonathan fumbles in his breast pocket and instead of the handkerchief there absently takes hold of the half-eaten lamb chop and offers it to her. The sudden gush of her laughter after initial amazement sets Jonathan also into a paroxysm of mirth which is further accentuated when he dumps the chop in an ashtray and suggests to an astonished waiter that he should add the item to his bill. 'I would never serve a lamb chop in an ashtray,' mumbles that worthy fellow defensively, and his dazed expression does little to diminish the frenzy of their enjoyment.

The laughter of a mischievous twain, bubbling like the effervescence of champagne while they writhe in their seats seems to suggest that they too were actually living the parts they played and found the whole situation screamingly funny. In a less hysterical way perhaps but equally conducive to laughter is Jonathan's attempts to dance the conga when he and Anne descend to the dance floor. It is a riotous exhibition and a space is cleared spontaneously by the other dancers who gather round to enjoy the spectacle of an ageing celebrity whose life had been despaired of only three weeks earlier cavorting around like a ten-year-old. Jonathan kicks and twists and turns as he enters into the fun of the occasion, bespeaking a surprising strength and agility in an old man. Few of the onlookers seem to doubt that his charming partner is responsible for the rejuvenation. It is a pity in a way that Johnny, accompanied by the omnipresent doctor, has to intervene to spoil the party. Johnny (stupid as ever, I thought, for his seeming indifference to Anne's physical attraction throughout much of the film is somehow unreal) promptly accuses Anne of low intrigue in luring his father to the night-club and endangering his health. When an indignant young lady throws the contents of a flute, Jonathan's cocktail of coconut milk plus nameless additives, in Johnny's face, thoroughly staining his evening garb in the process, one does not feel a shred of sympathy for him; on the contrary, that the act was just retribution for his insensitivity. As Anne firmly declares to him the next morning when the bead-twirler and her daughter, thanks to a newspaper headline that Johnny and Anne are engaged, have departed for Mexico – 'You deserved it and you got it.' But as may be imagined, there is forgiveness all round in the Reynolds household and reconciliation. This comes about after Jonathan feigns a fatal collapse to precipitate Johnny in headlong flight once again to the railway station to grab a disillusioned Anne as she is about to climb aboard a train bound for Ohio and her home town.

A most pertinent comment, and the last word I would say in an extraordinary situation, rests with an astounded railway porter. Twice within a week or two he has been obliged to hurl Anne's suitcases from a moving train. How can anyone not be wholly sympathetic when he yells after a girl who has twice failed to catch her train, 'The next time you ain't goin' no place I suggest you take a plane!'

Deanna Durbin

(Reproduced courtesy of The Movie Store Collection)

Chapter 12

The Amazing Mrs Holliday

Deanna's next film, 'The Amazing Mrs Holliday', was not released until 1943 after an interval of a year or more. Its theme is as sombre as many of its predecessors are light-hearted and frolicsome, although indisputably relevant to the contemporary mood at the time it came to the cinema screen. The fairy princess of 'First Love' and 'Spring Parade' has been transformed into a very practical young woman – Ruth is her Christian name in this story – who for much of her life has lived at a Christian missionary school in a remote Chinese village. As a consequence of the Japanese invasion of China she becomes ministering angel to eight orphaned children of different nationalities. Her uncle, founder and principal of the mission dies from injuries received in a Japanese air raid and it is Ruth's task to bring out the children to safety in the West. She does this by stowing away herself and her party on a ship bound for San Francisco – albeit not without the connivance and active help of a friendly ship's steward, an Irishman named Timothy. Her presence is discovered, however, by

Commodore Holliday, an old American sea-dog and ship's captain. But underneath his stern and indeed, more than forbidding exterior there beats, as future developments prove, a kindly and understanding heart. And though that veteran mariner soundly berates both Ruth and the steward whose responsibility for an illegal embarkation he does not for a moment doubt, he declares that he will ensure that all the orphan children will be admitted to the United States even if he has to adopt them himself to secure their entry. And that declaration is a vital argument which Ruth uses to advantage following her arrival in the States with her innocent fledglings. Not in the Commodore's ship, however, does she reach their coveted destination, for that is torpedoed en route, the commodore believed drowned, while the steward with Ruth and the children are rescued and transferred to another vessel bound for San Francisco.

Further complications await a missionary girl on arrival, not least of all the question of satisfying the Immigration authorities about identity and nationality. The children have no passports and though their refugee status is easily established, there are no funds available for their future support. Ruth's suggestion that she could open her own school and take care of them sounds incredibly naive to officials to whom the admission and welfare of a group of penniless immigrants in a strange land is not the simple formality Ruth has imagined it to be. Deanna herself, or rather Ruth, has American citizenship and is told that she is free to go her way but she has no relatives whom she can call upon for help. She looks distressed in her dismay so that her children, watching her very closely while she argues with officialdom, sense the predicament. The youngest, acutely sensitive, starts to cry, and that is a very good piece of professionalism in one so very young. A possible solution to the problem comes with the suggestion that the commodore's family who live in his luxurious mansion in San Francisco might be willing to pay a bond of 500 dollars in respect of each child – 4,000 dollars altogether – to secure their release. Off go Ruth and the steward on a mission which seems more fanciful than practicable. A penniless girl and eight little orphans seeking sanctuary is a proposition unlikely to commend itself to a household uncompromisingly staid – an elderly coterie of relatives more concerned with getting its hands on the commodore's considerable wealth than dispensing charity to a group of refugees.

Ruth and Timothy come in sight of the Holliday family home, an imposing mansion build in palladium style. They are overawed, the steward more than the girl, and their feeling is one of total inadequacy as they sense the reality of wealth and power and privilege, symbolised by the grandeur of the structure rearing before them in its extensive grounds.

An elderly butler opens the door to them and immediately wrinkles his nose, showing his disapproval of a nondescript old seadog and the nameless odours related to his calling. Nor, despite Ruth's good looks and diffident air, is he impressed by her dishevelled appearance. An old straw hat, a refractory curl trailing beneath it down her right cheek - a long, well-worn skirt with a hanging hem just above her ankles and a pair of heavy, black boots, give her a distinctly waif-like aspect. (But as a critic with a bias that nothing can influence I thought her whole appearance was one to arouse all the love and benevolence of which human beings are capable. Indeed, the drabness of her apparel coupled with her open-mouthed innocence as she surveyed the splendours of the main hall while the butler decamped to find out whether the mistress of the house would be willing to receive two unexpected visitors, was something which kindled my strongest protective instincts. I never saw any actress equal to Deanna's talent for registering surprise. It was so natural, so unfeigned. Her eyes would widen, the pupils dilate and a momentary rigidity of the cheek muscles would precede her smile, half-sweet, half-sheepish, but so beguiling in an involuntary way.)

The subsequent meeting with the inmates of the Holliday mansion initially seems hopeless, particularly when they scoff at the idea of facilitating the entry of eight immigrant children to the tune of 4000 dollars. A frustrated Timothy mournfully upbraids a selfish gentry, saying on impulse that he never thought to see Commodore Holliday"s kinsfolk turn away 'his own flesh and blood'. Ruth promptly backs him in the fiction of her marriage to the commodore at sea soon after her departure from China. It is thus that a very young widow becomes part of the Holliday clan together with her beloved orphans.

Seemingly securely established, Ruth avails herself of many of the advantages of Western civilisation in the matter of personal attire and cosmetic ornamentation and our next glimpse of her comes with her descending a sweeping staircase holding in one hand a whisky bottle (which she has confiscated from a bibulous steward) and a glass in the other. The transformation in her appearance is almost electrifying. The waif is gone, exorcised away by feminine ingenuity together with the fraying straw hat, the black boots and a torn skirt. Instead there is a dream of loveliness and apparent sophistication divinely coiffured and sheathed in a snowy white dress glittering with sequins. She contrives to move gracefully notwithstanding the encumbrance of a whisky bottle and glass and high-heeled shoes to which she is quite unaccustomed.

Who could blame the commodore's grandson, Tom, just arrived home from a long voyage and glancing casually up the stairway, for his gasp of astonishment at the sight of a beautiful stranger entering his field of vision?

Despite her physical attraction, the grandson suspects her of complicity in a plot to sieze the family inheritance when in response to his enquiry, 'Who are you?' she tells him she is Commodore Holliday's widow. 'That makes you my grandmother,' he remarks blandly - then with a cutting edge to his voice adds, 'What's your racket?' and almost in the same breath, "What's the pay-off?"

Ruth looks bewildered as well might a mission girl from the distant Orient confronted for the first time with a terminology quite strange to her, especially its connotations of wrong-doing. The grandson becomes sceptical to the point of derision when he is told furthermore that there are eight dependant children living in the mansion, all of them apparently the commodore's wards. But he is dumbfounded when they all come crowding down the stairway to throw themselves literally into Ruth's arms and smother her with their embraces. Ruth packs them off to bed with gentle persuasion before seating herself on the stair beside a junior Tom Holliday and giving an account of her past life.

The film continues with a series of flashbacks depicting Ruth at the Chinese mission school where she has lived through most of her childhood and throughout adolescence to young womanhood. We see her trim figure in outlandish garb - black jacket and loose trousers of matching shade - hair pulled back in a bun, ankles bare and wooden sandals or clogs shielding stockingless feet. Children crowd upon her, laughing, full of fun, and she skips along with them, that wayward, black curl, conspicuous in the early scenes of the film, flitting occasionally over her right eye. The emotional picture of a timeless and little known land torn by war is drawn with skill and imagination and though it panders to the traditional image in Western eyes of the mysterious East, the result is a passable verisimilitude.

Ruth sadly recalls the sudden impact of war on a peaceful community - the bombing of her village, the death of her uncle, the rescue of a Chinese baby from its dying mother, and the flight from a tormented land to safety. She leaves the commodore's grandson looking very thoughtful as she goes to tuck up the children. We are then treated to her rendering of 'Mighty Like A Rose' as she soothes a restless babe to sleep. The sound of her inspired and melodious voice penetrates to Tom's bedchamber and he and his butler find it so enthralling that they gaze at each other speechless. So restrained, so controlled are the throbbing strains of that lullaby, slightly tremulous and unutterably sweet. When they cease to flow as a restless child at last slips away into dreamland, the hush that follows brings with it a sense of painful valediction. In sharp contrast there is nothing mournful about the scene featuring a dinner party in the mansion where Ruth seems to be the guest of honour. Everyone waits upon her first mouthful. But Ruth fails to concentrate as she raises a cocktail cherry to her lips. It slips from her spoon and rolls along the table-cloth. All eyes are upon her as she tries to manoeuvre it into a position where she can scoop it up and restore it to a compote of fruit set before her. Up and down the table it rolls while she tries in vain to retrieve it. Once or twice she is tempted to pick it up in her fingers, only to see the butler, a dedicated believer in conformity, shake his head in a deprecatory manner. Eventually after all her fellow diners have watched an epic struggle with bated breath, Ruth decides to flout convention, delicately siezes the offending cherry with thumb and forefinger and pops it into her mouth. And good manners or not I can only comment that it was the most sensible thing to do.

Inevitably, as Tom begins to talk of a widow's inheritance and other family concerns, Ruth realises that her masquerade must soon come to an end lest she should suffer the embarrassment of being denounced as a fraud. She dons her old clothes and helped by a faithful Timothy tries to steal away in the lag hours of the night with the children in search of another refuge. But a party of hapless refugees, leaving all their new fineries behind and taking with them only the pathetic bundles with which they arrived, makes far too much noise descending the stairs and Tom is disturbed from sleep. He insists they stay until morning when Ruth can wait no longer and tells him the truth. He demands an explanation which leads to further flashbacks to China and the unravelling of facts about an illegal embarkation and its aftermath. Such intermission gives an opportunity for Ruth to sing a Chinese lullaby which she does in an indescribably tender way. Her interpretation of Oriental vowel sounds adds an unusual fascination to the tune. This is followed by a Chinese version of 'Hush-a'bye-Baby', the traditional vespers song perhaps for babies all over the globe.

The rest of the film perhaps is less an exercise in continuity than a series of very touching episodes which provide scope for Deanna's versatile acting. Under Ruth's soft persuasion Tom helps Ruth to settle the children for the night, for she has decided that as soon as the immigration papers arrive giving the children unconditional admission she will leave the Holliday mansion for good. But first she wants to assure herself that the orphans can be safely entrusted to Tom's care. Getting him to tuck them up in bed, she believes, is good preliminary training for an adoptive father. With Ruth's example to inspire him Tom shows real human warmth in the task and she is more than ever convinced of his fitness to become their protector in her place when he returns the spontaneous embrace of a little girl before settling her to sleep.

This is one of several occasions in the film when Ruth has to express the brooding sadness of one who faces the prospect of losing the beloved little ones she has rescued from a war zone and forfeiting a new found security and set forth alone to face an uncertain future. Shall I not say her performance is classical? Incidentally she plays the maternal role with such delicate sensitivity as to give more than an inkling of the devoted mother Deanna Durbin would become in her own personal life.

Not less affecting is the brief interlude in Ruth's bedroom when one of her female charges steals in simply to bid her 'goodnight'. Who can forget the lovely contours of her face as she gazes yearningly into the night from her bedroom window, and the sudden, impulsive hug for a tiny girl as she slips into bed.

Perhaps the most touching picture of all is that of Ruth singing in a quiet, upper room of a spacious mansion. Dressed after the fashion of a bygone age, with her eight children reclining on the floor about her, all in the frills and bows and ribbons of yesterday, she sings 'The Old Refrain'. Ruth looks stunningly attractive, but then I should add that her real-life mentor is beautiful all the time in every sense. And that includes the quality of an inner radiance which lights a glow in the eye and kindles a smile on the lips. Than this there is no surer sign of candour and the true spirit of selflessness.

I shall ever be at a complete loss whenever I try to put into words my feeling about those simple but heart-throbbing moments when Deanna, seated before a group of adoring children, sings with a full heart a song of unpretentious but soulful rapture. How easy it is to become emotional about such lines as

It was my mother taught me how to sing,
And to that memory I'll ever cling -
Never sad am I upon my way

You don't have to be a sentimentalist to appreciate the beauty and nostalgia of such rhyme. Nor, humming that dreamy tune repeatedly after hearing it for the first time, with my thoughts turned to memories and to loved ones gone from the world making one more deeply conscious of the blessing of true love oneself, was it difficult to adapt the melody and its metre to lines of my own composition such as:-

The past to me is still an open door;
I dream of loved ones gone for evermore;
And though my heart is sad I would not be
A stranger to their tender memory.

I see them smiling at me from afar,
A land that lies beyond the farthest star;
There is no shadow there, no mortal pain,
And there the joys we knew are born again.

And there is one whose ring rests on my hand,
Whose love is mine within that golden band –
God grant us that our laughter and our tears,
May not be lost in our eternal years.

The climax in the final scene of 'The Amazing Mrs Holliday' is magnificently contrived. A rich and glittering company is gathered in the commodore's mansion to participate in a 'China Ball' in aid of refugees from the war in the East. Ruth is a figure of exquisite charm and of dignified deportment a world apart from the dishevelled little waif of a few weeks earlier. She is positively a dazzling sight as she mounts a dais to thrill her listeners with an operatic aria which is received with a storm of applause. She is sheathed in white, is wearing star-shaped earrings and there are starry spangles in her hair. A simple circlet girds her neck and accentuates the splendour of the whole ensemble of a gorgeous dress and a delectable person.

The old commander, arrived back from the dead as it were - for it is axiomatic - plot-wise - that he has escaped drowning in the China seas - provides a tense moment for Ruth when he calls on the company to listen to something he has to say about a masquerade and a supposed young widow. At the last moment, however, he relents and claims the young woman as the wife he wed before his ship was torpedoed.

Unfortunately for Ruth and young Tom, who have belatedly confessed their love for each other, the commodore shows every intention of legitimising the union which is presumed to exist between himself and Ruth. Thankfully he shows good sense when privately informed by his family of the true situation between a prospective wife and his grandson. And so the film closes on a blissful note. The commodore adopts the eight orphan children and Ruth becomes the promised bride of a much younger and more romantic Holliday.

My final observation about 'The Amazing Mrs Holliday' must be that this film did not exactly depict a Deanna Durbin projecting the Spring-like gaiety which is associated with her films, but throughout its length, even through emotional and intimate moments, she maintained an air of dignity and self-possession. This quiet reserve, the kindly sense of detachment which is conventionally called 'mystique', was readily punctured by smiles and laughter when she was involved with the children who clung so close to her. During her career she may not have been the archetypal tragedienne, but in her serious roles she was a very convincing exponent of the dramatic art.

Chapter 1 3

Hers to Hold

Deanna Durbin's next film, 'Hers to Hold', was first screened in
July 1943. As in 'The Amazing Mrs Holliday', the story unfolds
against a background of war and the United States girding itself for a
life and death struggle against a ruthless foe. There is an abundance of
uniforms and matching personnel, soldiers flitting to and fro both on
duty and relaxation and battle hardware in the production stage. The
said hardware consists mainly of skeletal aircraft frames littering a high
assembly line in an equally cavernous factory which is a venue for
much of the action and practically all Deanna's vocal exertions.

In this film the Craig family featured in 'Three Smart Girls' and
'Three Smart Girls Grow Up' is resuscitated and makes its final bow.
Things have changed, however. Though the head of the family, Judson
Craig, looks much the same save for a few more wrinkles and grey
hairs, there is a new butler, new faces in the household and only the
youngest of three daughters, Penny, is left of a once mercurial and
often vociferous brood.

The film opens at a blood transfusion centre of the American Red

Cross. Bill Morley, a former American mercenary home from China, who has taken temporary employment in an aircraft factory while awaiting drafting into the Air Force, is attending the clinic to give blood, together with his friend, Rosey Blake. The two are relaxing on their beds when there is a sudden bustle among the nurses and auxiliary staff and a ripple of excitement runs through the ward. Orderlies hurry to and fro, having been told that a prominent socialite, Penelope Craig, a millionaire's daughter, is soon to attend as a blood donor. Everyone is full of speculation about a beautiful celebrity who is undoubtedly going to receive V.I.P. treatment. Reporters and photographers begin to crowd round the entrance to the ward, and soon Penny, hidden in the midst of a group of admirers, is ushered inside. A screen has been placed round the bed where Penny will undergo her transfusion.

After the hubbub and the flashlights Bill and his buddy strain their necks to catch a glimpse of the new arrival and Bill's imagination (his lust too in all probability) is stirred by the sight of a pair of shapely calves and ankles. The Craig family history seems to be well known to Rosey who explains that Penny is the last and youngest of three daughters at the parental home. Bill has a little book full of the addresses of the 'heart-throbs' of his past and professes surprise with tongue-in-cheek when he skims through the list and finds that Penny's name does not appear on it. That omission will have to be remedied is his reaction. A born philanderer, he thinks that every female fruit is ripe for plucking and Penny's much publicised physical attractions provide a stimulating challenge. He then overhears a medical orderly talking to the Craig girl while he performs the necessary transfusion. When a minor operation is finished the orderly says that he will personally bring Penny a glass of orange juice as a restorative. Thereupon a very presumptuous future recruit for the U.S. Air Force poses as a doctor, taking along with him his own orange drink for the purpose. His status is accepted by Penny without demur as she has no reason to challenge his authority. He asks for her address and telephone number as a double check for official records, and then takes a further liberty, checking her pulse, a routine matter, he says casually, taking her soft hand and admiring an expensive ring which, she remarks coyly, was a gift from her mother. Aware that he must leave Penny's private sanctuary before a real medical man returns, Bill impulsively implants a kiss on Penny's lips. She is naturally angry at his presumption and is not easily to be soothed by any excuses for an outrageous breach of etiquette by a professional person. Bill hurries off just as an innocent orderly returns with a glass of orange juice which he has promised a lady donor. He too takes Penny's pulse and then Bill, checking beyond the screen, hears him say, 'My, what a lovely ring!' Next – smack! – obviously Penny is in no mood for a repetition of a stolen kiss heralded by the same preliminaries. And, gathering up her belongings, Penny leaves the blood transfusion centre abruptly, feeling both indignant and insulted. When Bill leaves he makes no secret of the fact that he is more than keen to renew acquaintance with a beautiful young socialite and, although uninvited, decides to attend a party at the Craig residence.

(Such is the initial episode of a film which is an absolute delight throughout and in which Deanna is at her triumphal best both as an actress and singer. But, as the precursor of several other entertaining sequences, it is not to be excelled for humour and wit, which is my reason and excuse for recounting it in detail).

By the time Penny arrives home from the blood transfusion clinic the incorrigible 'Doctor' Morley is already on the telephone and she tells Binns the butler to 'hang up'. The party at the Craig mansion that evening is being held to celebrate an ageing magnate's umpteenth wedding anniversary. The person himself (dear old Charles Winniger as one might expect) is still as absent-minded as ever he was in 'Three Smart Grow Up'. He has even driven home in a car which is not his own but which happened to be parked in his own parking bay at his business headquarters. Far-fetched? Well – such exaggeration is acceptable in so pleasurable a context.

Also to be expected is Bill's gate-crashing of the party together with his less impetuous friend, Rosey Blake. Penny restrains her annoyance at his audacity and resolves to give Bill a taste of the medicine he so nonchalantly prescribes for others.

A very mature lady of some wealth and privilege, and an inveterate hypochondriac into the bargain, is persuaded by Penny that a certain Doctor Bill Morley might have a solution to her medical problem. But daringly he makes a diagnosis by the simple expedient of getting her to thrust out her tongue and scanning her gnarled features with deep interest. Nor is he particularly worried when Penny lures him into the company of a genuine doctor who is conspiring with Penny to teach him a lesson, a timely one for a cheeky upstart. Bill seeks to elude a determined hypochondriac who is trying to monopolise his attention, and he threads his way swiftly through a crowded room to escape her. Meanwhile Penny circulates among the guests singing 'Seguidilla' to the delight of many male admirers and at length catches up with Morley who has deftly eluded his tormentor. At the close of her song, gloriously rendered, she thrusts the stalk of a single rose between his lips to the amusement of onlookers. But he shrugs off any discomfiture. And his is the last word – for with Penny's parents watching open-mouthed and volatile guests fascinated observers – he seizes Penny in a close embrace and kisses her long and passionately.

That lingering salutation obviously has an effect upon Penny for in the next scene in a local dance club which is a rendezvous for aircraft workers and soldiery of all kinds we see a young socialite arrive, escorted by Rosey. Bill sees her appearance as an indication that his kiss has not alienated her completely but aroused perhaps an interest in his welfare. He feels himself drawn towards the dazzling beauty who has so suddenly entered his life and promptly deserts a regular girl friend in favour of Penny. He invites her to dance and her ready acceptance is a prelude to a situation which is perhaps more appropriate to slapstick comedy or farce than serious romance. There is only the merest touch of vulgarity, however, for Penny is decorously clad beneath her skirt. An upward draft presumably from a concealed vent in the dance-floor lifts Penny's hooped dress waist-high so that amid a gale of good-natured laughter she is obliged to withdraw and remove it, to return after a moment or two securely sheathed in a tight-fitting gown. The film redeems itself for an unexpected lapse, light-hearted though it was, with a subsequent tender love scene on a deserted beach whither Bill has taken Penny in quest of respite from a boisterous crowd of revellers. There follows a bit of cinema magic which would have been perfect in Technicolor – soft shades of a placid ocean and moonlit cloud and the starry eyes of lovelorn humans. Penny is hauntingly lovely as she gazes into Bill's face, her lips close to his. Talk is of the Milky Way and invisible worlds afar which leads him into musing on another consuming passion in his life – flying – like a 'pin-tailed widgeon' is his droll way of describing the operation. A military patrol who gently warn them that they are loitering within a prohibited area (the United States' eastern seaboard) brings their romantic dalliance to an end and it is back to the forecourt of the club restaurant, the sounds of lively music and jolly fraternisation. Bill, however, wary of too close an entanglement with the opposite sex – that 'forever and forever look in a girl's eye' is his picturesque euphemism for marriage – is non-committal about a further date. So Penny, resourceful as ever, becomes a 'working-girl' in the aircraft establishment in order to maintain her liaison with him. (Here I must remark that Penny's initial attempts to drill holes for rivets is a sight to broaden the smile on one's face. When she tentatively points a drill at a steel plate the foreman mutters scathingly, 'You don't shoot it – you drill it!'

In her search for Bill in a crowded concourse Penny is about to give up in despair when she meets Rosey. He has the bright idea of leading her up to a central platform or dais where the works band is playing during a lunchtime break. She understands that a song from her should enable Bill to locate her instead, for he has already heard her marvellous singing at the Craig party.

Rosey addresses a vast company and announces that a new member of the work force is about to sing for their enjoyment. This serves two purposes but I have no doubt that the primary one in the producer's mind was to enable Penny to give another enchanting performance. The song chosen is 'Begin the Beguine', which leads me to speculate how many of the millions for two generations or more who have heard it sung, as it should be sung by the well-trained voice of a great artist, have ever wondered about the meaning or significance of the word 'beguine'. In her role as Penny Deanna gives a rendition of extraordinary power and intensity – it is masterly both in its subdued intonations and the rise and fall of the liquid notes of melody. A fluctuating ride of bewitching sounds, passionate in crescendo, almost exultant in climax, has an almost mesmeric effect upon a huge assemblage of workmates. Its immobility while an inspired voice rings in an industrial amphitheatre is as profound as the rapt expression on every face turned towards the dais, eyes riveted on a girl not less lovely in overalls than a jewelled ball-gown, with a simple white kerchief binding her hair. (Deanna's performance was much, much more than merely memorable and in all her films it was with the most thrilling anticipation conceivable that I greeted her arrival on a dais before an assembled audience. Unlike the improvisations as to venue which its film script may call for, the ritualistic approach is essential in my view for a songstress of outstanding ability as Deanna was in her prime. Nothing could match that voice for commanding attention on and off the screen simultaneously.)

Despite the vow he has made to himself not to form too close an attachment to Penny, Bill realises that he is in love with her and he keeps a promise to call on her at her home while her father is engaged in showing home movies, a pleasure which the Craig family enjoys from time to time, especially a nostalgic journey into the past.

(Surprisingly the producers of 'Hers To Hold' took the opportunity of screening as an integral part of the film itself a few shots of Penny's days as a schoolgirl and adolescent. Thus we have the unexpected pleasure of catching a glimpse or two of Penny again as she appeared in 'Three Smart Girls'. She is once again singing in the stern of a trim sailing craft gliding across a Swiss lake before the blast of a horn summons her ashore. In the next flashback she is in her father's gymnasium in New York leaping into his arms. Then follows an anachronism which of course is forgivable – Penny (under a different name) riding a bicycle in the opening sequence of 'Mad About Music' and singing 'I love to Whistle' in the company of her classmates, and a further shot from the same film of a shy, young Austrian admirer presenting her with a box of chocolates. Two more excerpts follow – Penny having a bedroom tussle with her two sisters in 'Three Smart Girls Grow Up' and the second from 'It's a Date'. The flashbacks provide a brief, corporate enjoyment of several of Deanna's early and exhilarating films and just when one is beginning to wish that an impromptu cinema show within the story of 'Hers to Hold' could be prolonged indefinitely the film gets back on course.)

Bill arrives at the Craig mansion. He is in an odd mood, at first constrained, then finally, when Penny's parents have discreetly retired for the night, confessing his love for the girl and swearing that he will be true to her notwithstanding the uncertainties which the war might bring. Penny is ecstatically happy and she is seen in enchanting episodes when she goes out and about with Bill, one in which she tries her hand at the old Cumbrian pastime of 'gurning' (though such shapely facial contours as hers could never be made grotesque).

Comes the day when Penny mounts the dais in the huge aircraft hangar to sing with heart-throbbing, soulfulness and tender, patriotic fervour 'Say a Prayer for the Boys Over There'. In neat overalls without ostentation of any kind, dwarfed by her surroundings and a rapt multitude, she looks a tiny, vulnerable figure, kindling a protective instinct among the whole assembly. For as she sings it sees in her the embodiment of all it holds dear – of an America which must be kept inviolate at all costs. One feels the agony of tangled emotions – the collective pain and yearning of ordinary folk enduring separation from and fears for their kinsfolk and friends they love.

It is therefore understandable perhaps that when one of Penny's friends at work is notified of her husband's death in battle and stricken by grief collapses and is borne away, Bill decides that he cannot inflict such torment on his beloved Penny. Almost cruelly then he tells her that his love was all a mistake – that there is no future for them together.

Penny returns home and alone in her bedroom sings the 'Kashmiri Song' which is beautifully expressive of disillusionment, heart-break and despair. No songstress I have ever heard has interpreted that song with such sweet intensity, unravelling the misery and mystery of life when the human spirit seems to be on the verge of dissloution. The negation of hope and of trust, profound bewilderment and insufferable anguish of heart – Deanna expresses all these emotions with an astonishing realism. One feels that the intermittent sobs are not feigned in any sense, that she is fully experiencing the torment of unrequited love and a future shorn of all happiness or prospect thereof.

On the eve of his departure on a war assignment, however, Bill has second thoughts and asks his friend Rosey to act as intermediary with Penny. Rosey, alas, is barred from the Craig house by a father furious at the misery for which a fickle lover is responsible. Rosey contrives to transmit a written message to Penny via a sympathetic butler. Judson is suspicious of the butler's furtive behaviour and that devoted servant is obliged to slip the note into a sandwich to prevent the master getting his hands on it. The result of such subterfuge is hilarious. And to complicate the situation still further it seems that every guest in the house where a party is in progress designed to cheer Penny up, is smitten by a desire to lighten the butler's tray as he offers the sandwiches round a crowded chamber. Penny herself tries to follow the tray around and repeatedly helps herself to a sandwich in an effort to locate the scribbled note. The camera switches to each guest in turn to determine from his or her expression if the first mouthful unearths something unexpected and at the same time Penny anxiously scans the room waiting for the tell-tale commotion which will signal the end of a paper chase. It is Judson who eventually discovers the missive lurking in his smoked salmon. Thankfully still legible are the few words declaring Bill's love and his wish to see her.

And so ensues a happy ending, although with the usual Hollywood insistence on maintaining suspense until the last possible moment, it is not till Bill is on the point of entering an airport channel leading to an exit and a military aircraft revving just beyond that a breathless Penny calls his name. A tender leave-taking and a final rendering by Penny of 'Say a Prayer for the Boys Over There' in front of her assembled workmates bring the film to a close.

Deanna singing as only she can against a backdrop of dark and silver clouds flowing deceptively into the furthest reaches of the sky is the kind of haunting vista which conjures thoughts about the miracle of life itself in a Void symbolising Eternity, and poses the question whether love born of mortality, however deep and abiding, can outlast it.

'Hers to hold' is a predominantly happy film – a sombre interlude now and then does but serve to accentuate the atmosphere of gaiety. The theme is the better for the ennobling tear and optimism is not muted by occasional misgiving. The lofty reflection induced by the closing scene adds an idealistic touch which is not a mere patina of make-believe.

Chapter 14

His Butler's Sister

If I had to choose from the full list of Deanna's films the one which gives me the greatest pleasure in respect of her singing it would undoubtedly be the one first screened in November 1943, namely, 'His Butler's Sister'. My reason is a simple one. In no other film does she sing four such glorious songs as 'In the Spirit of the Moment' (despite the novel circumstances in which the rendition takes place), secondly, 'When You're Away', an inspired love-song, next 'A Russian Medley' in a very appropriate and festive atmosphere, and lastly, the thrilling aria 'None Shall Sleep' from Turandot which her brilliant soprano voice brought to pulsing life. Time and time again have I listened to that refrain, both sad and joyous, sung with a perfection none has ever equalled. And I am sure that opinion is shared by many others, near or afar, who have been fortunate enough to hear it. Oh, begone, Pavarotti!

The story of the film which has the semblance of a fairy-tale is a straightforward one or, should I say, uncomplicated. There are no sudden twists and turns in the plot, just a simple progression of incidents which prompt speculation as to whether the heroine who is a singer of great potential will achieve her ambition of making a successful career for herself in opera. For such aspiration is deftly side-stepped by the film's producers in favour of a more romantic theme, her growing attachment to a celebrated composer and the gradual blossoming of love actuated as much by his professional competence in an art closely related to her own talent as his handsome profile. Yet I cannot wholly believe that one, be he genius or no, who exhibits a facile charm and on occasions can be downright surly and unmannerly, is worthy of the regard, much less the adulation, of a very sweet and sensitive girl. There are in my view only two occasions when Charles Gerard, the composer, really gives the impression that he is captivated by an adorable and sometimes delightfully naive girl – firstly, when about to bid her goodbye after dismissing her from his domestic staff, he sees her beautifully dressed for a ball, her lovely face shadowed by a wistful sadness and unfulfilled longing; and secondly, in the closing moments of the film when she is singing 'Nessun Dorma' from Turandot. Noting the signs of distress in her look, he moves towards the stage where she is performing, his face expressive of deep and tangled emotion, concern, contrition, the revelation that he has at last traced the elusive voice which has long enthralled him but which he has never been able to identify with a specific individual, and finally the reciprocal love which she has long hoped for.

(My own feeling is that Deanna's youthfulness and surpassing charm called for the sort of appreciation and enthusiasm which she received from actors of a similar age to her own and with whom she was called upon to share romance. As an actress she exemplified all that is fresh and innocent and wonderful in life – the time of youth and the eternal joy of Spring. If she was worthy even of idolatry as much for her appearance, her spiritual being and her artistic talent, then the proper vehicle for its expression was ideally a partner young enough to be free of the cynicism and perhaps the disillusion about life which so often taints the predispositions of the mature man of the world. He is the man of experience and sophistication who might well be more disposed to welcome to his arms someone who will warm his slippers and become slave to his whims rather than a girl still harbouring dreams of romance, and as Deanna herself sang in her earliest film, 'someone who will never scold her but watch over her and take care of her.')

In the film Deanna is Anne Carter and the composer is played by Franchot Tone. We are introduced to him, Charles Gerard, very early in the story when both he and Anne are travelling by chance on the same train, New York bound. He has already given a porter strict instructions to prevent stage-struck girls from invading his compartment. As a consequence, when Anne learns from two other disappointed hopefuls of his presence on the train and proposes to seek him out and sing for him, a wily porter directs her to another compact drawing-room. 'You might try drawing-room A,' he says, smiling broadly.

Deanna Durbin and Franchot Tone in 'His Butler's Sister'.

(Reproduced courtesy of The Movie Store Collection)

Drawing Room A is occupied by a middle-aged salesman who specialises in ladies' underwear. He evinces wide-eyed surprise when a lovely girl seeks admittance and who, convinced she is addressing Charles Gerard, asks politely if she can sing for him. Almost in a trance at the sudden interruption and extraordinary request he nods his head affirmatively and listens without saying a word as she moves close to a window table and bursts into song. 'In the Spirit of the Moment' is a number composed by Gerard himself, and she is still in the midst of a session of lilting melody when the train draws into a station where the composer alights. Though he hears her voice ringing down the platform and he is very intrigued, the train moves off before he is able to catch sight of the singer herself. Anne is dismayed when she realises the real trade of her auditory. He opens a suitcase and draws forth an article of feminine wear which is not designed for public viewing. Anne promptly flees his compartment. However, Destiny rules that her introduction to Gerard is not to be long delayed. Her brother, Martin, who is much older then herself and with whom she intends to stay awhile, turns out to be Gerard's butler. Anne is bound for the penthouse where he works. He has previously sent her a thousand dollars which he came by through a straight bet on a horse (or should it be 'mare') named 'Little Sister', a fact which presumably turned his thoughts to a sister whom he has not seen for ten years since he left home in the American heartland for the big city. Having spent all her money on clothes her intention is to lodge with Martin in New York while she endeavours to find some influential composer or impresario who may give her a start in the world of musical entertainment. The unexpected gift of a thousand dollars has convinced her that her brother is a rich man, especially since he lives in Park Avenue. She has no suspicion that he is just an employee, the servant of another – to wit, a butler.

She is very downcast when he tells her of his true status but thrilled to discover that fate has directed her to Gerard's penthouse suite in a fashionable quarter. All her attempts to sing for the composer, however, are frustrated, although with the help of Gerard's elderly house-keeper, Serafina, she does manage to insinuate herself into his service as a maid. Gerard himself finds her presence congenial but he gives no overt sign that he is sensible of her physical attractions. On the other hand, a group of older men, butlers from establishments in the rich apartment block, do not trouble to disguise their feelings and almost fawn upon Gerard's lovely new maid, helping her collectively with her shopping and each spurning the other in their eagerness to bask in her smile if not to win her favours. So do the male friends of the composer at a party in his suite when they desert their ladies to wait upon the maid in the kitchen. Only the disapproving glances of Ann's brother Martin who is afraid that his sister might compromise his own position as butler, sours a cheerful and fascinating episode. His insistence that she should maintain a 'deadpan' results in Ann screwing up her features while serving refreshments to the guests. Her droll look makes them wonder and causes some concern, until she helps a film producer present to get rid of his hiccups and relaxes thereafter with a radiant smile. There is a whisper from a previously very puzzled lady, 'She's beautiful', as once again her miserable brother interrupts the revelry and waves her dismissively to the kitchen.

The film continues with a succession of amusing incidents and one or two when the sentiment becomes serious. For instance, the brother persuades Gerard to dismiss his sister as surplus to requirements in a small household when the composer contemplates leaving New York for Maine to join a lady who has been trying to ingratiate herself with him. Ann is interviewed by a producer with amorous proclivities and while she is fending off his advances Gerard enters and is considerably taken aback when he recognises his former maid. He virtually ignores her while he explains to the producer that he is abandoning his career for an indefinite period and leaving New York. Ann is moved to tell him that she thinks he is making a mistake and one which he will regret, before she makes a dignified exit. The producer and Gerard gaze after her in disbelief and wonderment, amazed by her poise and the seeming emergence of a new personality, no longer that of a lowly maid but one prepared to face life's future challenges unflinchingly, alone if necessary, and above all one confident of her destiny.

Perhaps the film's most enthralling sequence apart from the thrilling climax takes place in a local restaurant called the Troika, a popular rendezvous of exiled Russians, where a party is held to celebrate the birthday of one of Ann's admirers, Popov, a Russian. It is primarily a gathering of friends where unstinted eating and drinking and merrymaking is the programme for an evening of celebration. It is in this spacious venue that Ann startles everybody when she bursts spontaneously into song while a Russian orchestra and vocal group provide a superb accompaniment to Ann's inspired singing. Indeed, a medley of folk-songs is concluded amid a storm of applause from an enraptured crowd while her astounded brother folds her in his arms. 'Why didn't you tell me you could sing like that?' he protests, and with gurgling laughter she replies 'I tried to.' There never was a more touching moment in the film, and one almost felt grateful that Martin should at last exhibit a spark of real human feeling which hitherto had been conspicuously absent in his treatment of Ann.

As might be expected, Gerard has second thoughts about going on vacation and is bent on seeing Ann again. But he arrives belatedly at the restaurant and therefore is not witness to her splendid performance. She accepts his invitation to dance, however, and does so to the music of his own composition 'In the Spirit of the Moment'. They desert the party and adjourn to another night-club before they make their way back on foot to the penthouse.

When the twain declare their love for each other you can be forgiven for thinking that at last true love has found a way. Not a bit of it, because an impressionable Gerard is inveigled by Martin into believing that Ann is a crafty lass making a pretence of love to further her desired career. An incredibly foolish and obtuse composer proceeds to taunt Ann and thanks her sarcastically for an entertaining evening.

All misunderstandings are cleared up in the last act at a 'Butler's Ball' where Gerard, who has suspected close links between Ann and the butler unconnected with a blood relationship, learns from Serafina that they are brother and sister. So to a heart-warming climax.

Here let me add that it is one of my pleasures when I have

watched a film of Deanna's ending with the traditional, soulful embrace of dedicated lovers, to imagine a possible sequel. As an example of this, 'His Butler's Sister' is the one which springs most readily to mind with its closing shot of a tearful but smiling Ann Carter hastening from the stage and falling into the arms of a mesmerised Gerard to the obvious delight of onlookers who crowd upon the enamoured couple. I visualise them disengaging from each other and threading their way through the press to a secluded table. He is full of praise for her singing. Their talk is intimate and joyous, their mood mercurial and loving. Ann refers to the laughable incident involving a 'girdle-man' – and her rendering of 'When You're Away' in his own apartment. He is at last able to link her with the voice on the train and the one he believed was issuing from a radio outside his dressing-room. 'If only I had known' he will probably say but later confess that there is something more important than her career, namely his love for her. Very soon comes the inevitable question, 'Ann, will you marry me?' And in her lustrous eyes he will read the hoped-for acceptance. Later, at a reception in his apartment attended by Popov and his fellow butlers, Gerard will ask the once intractable Martin as Ann's nearest surviving relative to give the bride away. But he will grin wryly and remark that it would not be exactly convenient for Martin to continue serving as butler in his household. He will suggest that the other should help him in the management of Ann's career as a singer if it is still her wish to make a name for herself. And he will probably inform the faithful Serafina that despite what he said at the 'Butlers' Ball' when, having learned from her that Martin and Ann were brother and sister and not lovers as he had assumed, he was so relieved that he had expressed his willingness to eat fish *ad nauseum* and love it, he did not want her to serve fish at his wedding breakfast.

Such an extension of the original story might not rival the emotional climax of two lovers sweeping into a tender embrace to general applause and approbation, but it might satisfy a sense of something missing when details implicit in a plot are glossed over – too many words which would assuredly be spoken in everyday life are left unsaid. I grant you that to adhere too closely to what might be termed normality might imperil the fairy-tale plot itself. Questions or suppositions therefore must be ignored, even at the risk of credulity. To take that conspicuous example for instance to which I have already referred – in 'His Butler's Sister' when Ann, a little anxious about her future following notice of her dismissal, seats herself at one of Gerard's two pianos and sings with a full heart 'When You're Away' to demonstrate her vocal talents. We have to believe that Gerard is under the impression that the voice is emanating from a portable radio in his dressing-room. Ann is performing in the atrium outside and a closed door would surely have muffled the sound to a degree to make a person with normal hearing speculate as to its source. It is difficult to accept such a possibility even for cinematic purpose and the continuity of the story. The fiction is prolonged still further in the subsequent scene. Having finished her song, Ann hears movement next door and rises from her seat fully expectant that Gerard is about to enter the music-room and will enthuse over her singing. But he is quite dis-passionate and seems more concerned with the portable radio he is carrying than a very attractive girl puzzled by his failure to show any response at all to a song he undoubtedly must have heard. Noting Ann's glazed expression he asks, 'Is there anything wrong?' Why on earth did Ann not reply, 'Didn't you like my singing, then?'

In the ordinary, mundane atmosphere of normal life such a query would have been the instant reaction of a splendid vocalist, proud of her voice, who had just poured out her heart in a thrilling way. She might even have thought to herself – 'Is he deaf? What does he want – blood!' Presumably then even a seemingly obtuse composer would have realised (by renewed demonstration of a maid's talent if he had deemed that necessary) that he had indeed been listening to the same voice that had charmed his ear on a railway platform when Ann, all unwitting of an extramural interest, had blithely sung 'In the Spirit of the Moment'.

Of course, such revelation would have entailed the abandonment or amendment of the original plot, perhaps also the romantic interludes of Popov's party and the nocturnal perambulations of a couple learning about each other's past and conscious of the beginnings of deep love for each other. To be fair one must ask the question – would not such revision have destroyed the feeling of joyous expectation about the revealing to a composer of Anne's talent in the musical field, in particular in the final act when, hearing the announcement that 'Miss Ann Carter will sing an aria from Turandot' he exclaims in his ignorance, 'What, here – in front of all these people?'

And so from a purely aesthetic point of view it is best to consider 'His Butler's Sister' as an exercise in romanticism which gave tremendous and lasting pleasure to a wide audience, as it will always do given that the more cultured of human susceptibilities are not prone to change. Therefore I must needs recant and admit that although it is fascinating to speculate what action might have followed the interpolation of a few words in a plot, it is best after all to leave such words unsaid – perhaps the wisest course for a script-writer to pursue if a fairy-tale is to come true in a singularly dramatic way with acclamations and rejoicing as befalls in 'His Butler's Sister'. Nor can I sensibly deny that such a theme, both creative and imaginative, makes for splendid theatre!

Chapter 15

Christmas Holiday

Deanna Durbin's fourteenth film, 'Christmas Holiday', released not long after 'D' Day in 1944, is the very antithesis of 'His Butler's Sister' in mood and style, above all in the characters it sets out to portray.

Appropriately enough for the sombre times in which it was released, it opens with a military parade in a wartime camp where a newly commissioned army officer is about to go on leave to marry. Although he is notified at the last moment that a faithless lover has already married another he decides nevertheless to proceed to his original destination, presumably to remonstrate with his ex-fiancée while accepting a *fait accompli* – which on the face of it would seem a very stupid thing to do.

Just why it was necessary to involve him in affairs of the heart incidental rather than essential to the script becomes apparent when the plane taking him to San Francisco where his faithless sweetheart dwells encounters a severe gale en route and he is obliged to divert to New Orleans. The delay means that our hapless lieutenant has to stay

110

overnight in that legendary city. It is there that a blasé newspaper reporter, cynical like so many in his profession, introduces him to the hostess of a night-club who, behind a facade of conventional hospitality, is a not unwilling procuress. She introduces the lieutenant to Jackie Lamont (our Deanna), a singer at the club whose past history has been laced with misfortune. The army officer's unrequited love is easily to be correlated with Jackie's own experience in that field. Now we understand that a jilted soldier is simply the instrument by which a torch-singer's unhappy past is to be unveiled – not a future lover for her in her bleak loneliness of heart, but a well-disposed observer. Our initial hopes of a promising liaison between Jackie and the lieutenant are therefore quickly dissipated. There is apparently no body chemistry between the two. Jackie is quite dispassionate and mournful in turn when they have a drink together and dance following Jackie's rendition of a typical cabaret number, 'Spring Will Be a Little Late This Year'. And that leads me to reflect that the lyrics in this film, tuneful though they may be, are almost wholly subjective in character. The music, like the desolate humans responding to its rhythms, mimes to the prevailing gloom and melancholy. The Midnight Mass in a majestic cathedral which Jackie attends escorted by a sympathetic lieutenant, superbly portrays Man's submission to an Eternal God, rich in reverence and solemn in exegesis. But even that is no incentive for rejoicing or for Jackie to shake off her depression. Missa Choralis and Adestre Fidelis offer no choral delight for her. She weeps unrestrainedly, seated within a cavernous nave and surrounded by soaring marble columns which seem to symbolise the dominance rather than the compassion of the Almighty. Jackie's uncontrolled sobbing affects her companion deeply, but he remains silent and solicitous. With Jackie still in a distressed state after the service they adjourn to a coffee-stall serving simple refreshments and, fairly composed at last, Jackie talks about her past. As with 'The Amazing Mrs Holliday' this is another occasion in Deanna's films in which flashbacks are used to clarify the storyline and to explain how a refined and cultured young woman, by all accounts once happily married, has sunk to a degraded level, singing in a night-club of dubious reputation. For the whole atmosphere of the place is suggestive of clandestine pleasures and dance hostesses not unwilling to gratify the carnal desires of male patrons given the right consideration.

(To my mind flashbacks in any film interrupt the continuity of a story or retard the current action. But I accept that they become essential in 'Christmas Holiday' if only to soften the shock of seeing our beloved Deanna in a rather demeaning role and present it in a way which will stir our compassion instead of inviting our strictures. Could it be true? Our princess of light and laughter in a drinking-den, a prey to the bold scrutiny of clients lacking in the social graces and not simply bent on an evening's entertainment with frivolous gossip and carousal? Perish the thought! Jackie must be presented in the most favourable light in pandering to our expectations. No hint should there be of risky flirtation – certainly not casual prostitution. The assumption is that the director of the film is still mindful of the legend that a younger Deanna created – the fairy-tale of perennial Spring and lasting innocence or naiveté, sullied only by a chaste kiss or two.)

Be that as it may, Jackie's excursions into her past which punctuate the unfolding film, are poignant in a stark contrast of black and white, light and shadow subtly interwoven, as she follows a domestic trail fraught with hazard. Her real name is Abigail and it is her misfortune to have met a young man at a concert with whom she later becomes friendly. She tells him that whenever she listens to good music something is added to her life which was not there before, which is elementary logic I suppose. (Anyway, however imperfectly expressed, it is a sentiment which all filmgoers who are disciples of the living Deanna share in equal measure whenever they have the good fortune to see one of her films.)

Jackie's misfortune in making a friend of the stranger she meets at the concert becomes all too clear in the events which follow. The friend, Robert Minette, tells Abigail, which is her name at that point, that he comes of an old family of much repute in New Orleans and that great things are expected of him as the bearer of a proud title. That may sound an extravagant expectation and it is assuredly the apogee of maternal hopes for a son of whose vices and waywardness Robert's widowed mother, unlike poor Abigail, is well aware. For to Abigail's dismay Robert proves to be a wastrel of the worst kind, an inveterate gambler and a petty criminal – he is unutterably selfish despite the avowal of love which leads her into marriage. At first his mother is overjoyed that her son is committed to a girl who loves him in return, and six months of seemingly blissful happiness follow for the wedded pair. The joy and serenity of their lives in this deceptive interlude is aptly illustrated in a scene in which Abigail sits at a piano and sings the song 'Always' very emotionally, watched by Robert and a mother who is almost pathological in her love for an undeserving offspring. On the surface, anyway, Robert appears to have mended his ways. He no longer frequents a seedy cafe which was one of his old haunts – a drinking-den for bookmakers and compulsive gamblers. Then comes Abigail's dramatic discovery that her husband's evil traits have not been exorcised away by her tender devotion and love. She sees his mother putting a blood-stained pair of trousers into an incinerator. Robert's gambling debts and the demands of creditors have resulted in his murdering one of his tormentors. The police are soon on his track. He goes to trial, is convicted and sent to prison. His distracted mother most unfairly blames Abigail for not doing more to keep him out of mischief. She is in fact brutal in her condemnation of Abigail and slaps the girl's face forcibly, crying, '<u>You</u> killed him!' – which is sufficient to inculcate poor Abigail with an irrational sense of guilt.

Grieving and inconsolable, Abigail leaves the Minette home and drifts into a new and unsavoury way of life as a dance hostess and torch-singer. The memory of Robert, however, and the hope of reunion when he has served his prison sentence, sustain her in her trials. Her love for an unrepentant criminal seems not to waver.

With flashbacks at an end, the film resumes with a telephone call to the army lieutenant at his hotel to the effect that with the weather soon to clear he may expect to embark at midnight for San Francisco.

(At this point, with the lieutenant's departure imminent, I abandon the hope that there might be a chance of him and Jackie conceiving a sudden liking for each other. After all, why should not love grow out of his respect for the dignity, if not the fatalism, which is always in her mien despite her mental torture and despair. That, I reason, would be an ideal way of salving the spiritual hurt which affects both their lives. Somerset Maughan, however, rules otherwise.)

Jackie's depraved husband breaks jail and makes for the night-club where his wife works. He is well briefed, no doubt by his bemused mother, about Jackie's, or to him, his Abigail's, new mode of living, but places the worst possible construction upon her activities in the club. With the intellectual sleight-of-hand for which Hollywood is renowned, Robert has acquired a hand-gun which he proposes to use upon the unwitting Abigail, notwithstanding her protestations of love and fidelity. One almost sighs with relief when a vigilant policeman, nimble on the draw, despatches a pathetic psychopath from this world. Not unexpectedly Abigail herself is grief-stricken and falls sobbing on her dying husband. This wise 'Christmas Holiday' reaches its doomladen end. The valedictory cry from the well-meaning lieutenant who is on hand to bid Abigail goodbye before leaving San Francisco, 'You can let go now, Abigail,' hopefully foretells the rejuvenation of a torn spirit. But Abigail raises a tear-stained face to heaven as though seeking the lost soul of her dead spouse beginning its everlasting journey. But indeed, were such transfiguration possible I cannot conceive of anyone less deserving of it than the abominable Robert. Nor can I believe that the Deanna of real life would ever have put faith in such a monster.

Here let me say that the title of the story, 'Christmas Holiday', misled me initially when I first saw it on film posters. I imagined straightaway a light-hearted romance with touches of pure comedy after the fashion of 'Spring Parade' and 'It Started With Eve'. There would be the glamorous setting of a winter and ski resort, sleigh rides beneath the moon and a radiant Deanna thrilling the night with joyous, lilting song. I imagined her muffled in a warm cloak trimmed with white fur sweeping along by a frozen lake – snow-covered peaks afar and fairy lights of all colours twinkling in a village ahead, a village where Christmas festivities were in full swing. A musical extravaganza in the true Deanna Durbin tradition would end with our beloved songstress giving us the immortal, 'Silent Night – Holy Night', not a subdued version as in 'Lady On a Train', but a rendition with full orchestra, not to be excelled for sweetness of tone, haunting intonation and a marvellously controlled power of expression.

Alas, the actual 'Christmas Holiday' I saw for the first time soon after the war of 1939/45 ended, was a concept totally different in character and style to the one I had fondly envisaged. There must have been millions of filmgoers like myself who saw its showing, if not with something akin to dismay, at least with mixed feelings. Deanna's singing of 'Always' was an absorbing experience. But the story itself and its miserable ending was thoroughly depressing. I thought Deanna acted throughout splendidly. But for me the part of Abigail was not the right vehicle for her special talents. Her personality itself is an evocation of Spring. One such as she should skip amongst flowers in full bloom, not shuffle among the dead leaves of winter. In 'Christmas Holiday' Deanna demonstrated what a versatile actress she was during her career. But the story line is morbid, and lacked even a *soupçon* of that blessed escapism which was the largesse Deanna dispensed so freely in most of her other films. Furthermore, that mesmeric song 'Always' was worthy of a venue much more inspiring than a sleazy night-club, a dreary drinking-parlour with a barely concealed aura of debauchery. I can only observe that it was both a happy and fortuitous circumstance that Deanna had little to do with the morose Mr Maughan – an apostle of misery if ever there was one – until she had made many of the exhilarating films in her true image, the miracle of Springtime. For, as a classic writer of ancient time would have written – Deanna is a daughter of the gods, and goddesses are not made to suffer human sin.

Chapter 16

Can't Help Singing

'Can't Help Singing', Deanna's next film which had its premiere in the same year as 'Christmas Holiday', was the only film in which she appeared in colour. With Jerome Kern supplying the music for a splendid outdoor romp set in the old Wild West of America I fully expected to have the pleasure of listening to the most tuneful songs imaginable. Nor was I disappointed. The song, 'Can't Help Singing', which provides a titular introduction to the film itself and 'Any Moment Now', sung against an idyllic backdrop of mountain and forest, were perfect examples of the kind of mellifluous sound and lyricism which was a hallmark of Deanna's films. The opening scene of a lone rider galloping across a scorched plain while hill and ravine lie stark under a torrid sun might well support the impression that here was an outrider of an army contingent on its way to chastise the unruly Indian. One expected to behold an ebullient Custer soon to surge into view, his yellow locks streaming in the breeze. Nothing so romantic, however. He is simply a messenger involved in the first shipment of gold from California to Washington.

116

Deanna Durbin in 'Can't Help Singing'
(Reproduced courtesy of The Movie Store Collection)

Anyway, a newspaper headline flashing across the screen leaves us in no doubt as to his mission. But time moves on at a headlong pace in the realm of the cinema and the camera switches instantly to the steps of the Capitol in Washington where, beneath the Stars and Stripes blowing in the wind, a military band as flamboyant as it is percussive is playing to a crowd of soldiers and civilians. The President of the United States himself is the central figure on a dais and is surrounded by senators and congressmen and the inevitable civil service administrators of high rank.

Across the parade-ground through the heart of a colourful assemblage rides an army captain who, amid much acclamation and excitement, proffers to the presidential hand the first bag of gold nuggets from the far West. The President launches into a patriotic speech but long before its conclusion Deanna (parading this time as Caroline, daughter of a prominent senator) makes an impressive entry into the film. She is gorgeously dressed in nineteenth century costume which exemplifies the sartorial sense of feminine forbears, and lightly as with expert hand she holds the reins in a buggy pulled by a sprightly pair of horses. She looks a perfect picture of youthful charm and innocence with her braided hair and a hat bedecked with green ribbons fluttering in the breeze. The horses advance at a rhythmic trot as Deanna (nay, Caroline) pours out her heart in song. 'Can't Help Singing' is a lyrical creation which is more than merely melodious, and sung by Caroline it is a virtuoso performance. Its reprise on several occasions during the film simply enhances the delicious memory of an inspired songstress.

Caroline has earlier been banished to the country-side by her father but she is now bound for the gathering at the Capitol in defiance of his wishes. We learn that there is a cavalry officer in town of whom she is fond, but whom her parents dislike intensely as an opportunist and self-seeking adventurer. So, much to their annoyance and dismay they catch sight of Caroline together with the young man as the concourse disperses, and propose to give him short shrift. Caroline's father in particular is angered by a rather conceited and arrogant suitor for his daughter's hand. A self-styled fiancé adopts a conciliatory tone to no avail. The senator is quite dismissive. Caroline is more than resentful of his abruptness towards her cavalry officer and is outraged by a parental lecture about her liaison with him. Her stern father tells her that she must sing at a presidential party soon to be held since she has chosen to return to Washington.

The resourceful Caroline promptly feigns illness – for good measure she presents that for some unaccountable reason she has lost her voice, and she takes to her bed with a hot water bottle to raise her temperature and perpetuate the fiction of laryngitis.

(In an ensuing harangue with the senator we are treated to a glimpse of Deanna in frilly pantaloons. She is still able to look decorous but nevertheless she is a stimulating sight. In retrospect I feel that there was a degree of intimacy about that exposure reminiscent of a bedroom scene in 'Three Smart Girls Grow Up' in which Deanna is warming her nightie in front of a fire before plunging into a warm cot. It also reminds me of the attractive girl sheathed in silk pyjamas who tumbles out of bed in 'Because of Him' and later stands obediently in front of Charles Laughton who blandly observes that whenever the press are seeking a photograph of them together they always seem to be coming out of bedrooms.)

Caroline sobs uncontrollably when her father informs her that a certain cavalry officer has been despatched to the distant West, but like a typical materialist he seeks both to console her and persuade her to accept his way of thinking by recourse to his wallet. A new outfit and some feminine fripperies, he reasons, will assure her compliance. Then off he goes to the President's party, fully expecting his daughter to follow, especially now that he has discovered that Caroline's sudden illness was a sham. She seizes the opportunity to pack her bags – one a very large trunk – and to hurry west in pursuit of her lieutenant whom she believes she loves.

And so a capricious young woman disappears from the parental home and a distracted father, more concerned for her safety than angry at her disobedience, posts a reward of five thousand dollars for information as to her whereabouts.

Following a western trail Caroline is next seen in a town called 'Independence'. She is immaculate as ever as the debutante daughter of a rich senator should be. Her sojourn in what used to be called 'a one-horse town', though brief, is full of incident, some of it improbable but highly comical. But nothing is more delightful than Caroline singing in a capacious bath-tub, her nudity wholly concealed by bubbling foam as she soaps herself. In an adjacent cubicle of a communal bath-house a roaming cowboy and gambler named Johnny starts singing the same song, 'Can't Help Singing'. His is a rich tenor voice which complements Caroline's warbling admirably. Their duet is unforgettable, a feast of glorious harmony, even when Johnny improvises his own words to accompany the melody. Caroline's blonde, braided locks are a joy to behold, just as alluring as those of the debutante in 'A Lady On A Train'.

Caroline and Johnny are destined to be thrown together when they argue over five hundred dollars which she has paid to a confidence trickster (the girdle-man of 'His Butler's Sister') who then parted company with that dishonest acquisition when he lost it gambling with Johnny in a noisy saloon. Johnny disputes possession until he discovers that Caroline is the missing heiress. He decides to claim the five thousand dollar reward for her return to her family. But Caroline, resourceful as ever, offers him a much larger sum if he agrees to keep quiet about her identity and serve as her escort on the western trail. The reason she gives for such a journey is that she is pledged to marry the landowner and magnate, Jake Carstairs, richest man in California.

Thereafter, amid all the comings and goings in a riotous affair there are several sequences featuring two immigrants from Eastern Europe, allegedly with royal affiliations, who turn out to be common thieves, trying to make off with Caroline's trunk. But they always end up in the same wagon in a train of such vehicles bound for California.

One of the funniest incidents in the whole film, if not the funniest, occurs when Caroline, still wearing all her finery and sleeping softly on a blanket beside her wagon, stirs from rest as dawn breaks over a western horizon. (And that is not a repudiation of natural phenomena, the horizon in question pertaining to Mid-West America). She opens her eyes to find a crowd of Indians in traditional costume looking upon her in wonder. But her scream is electrifying and in one concerted movement a tribal gathering suddenly turns in its tracks and flees panic-stricken across a parched plain. The two would-be thieves take fright too, inadvertently going in the same direction as the Indians until they realise their mistake. They are still clinging tenaciously to Caroline's trunk. The whole sequence is one to be viewed with tongue-in-cheek, but who would cavil at an improbability when a musical comedy is performed with a zest which is sustained throughout and includes moments of delirious fun.

The closing scenes of the film illustrate Hollywood's showmanship at its best. Romanticism never wavers and we are once again emphatically in the realm of spectacular pageantry and renewed confirmation of the artistry and loveable traits of the principal star. On the last stretch to California when Caroline has gone ahead to a fort where she hopes to find the cavalry officer she is really pursuing, we find a disconsolate Johnny missing her presence acutely. To be sure he is conscious of sweet pangs of love for a beautiful socialite, whatever the unpredictability of her ways. Abruptly he leaves the wagon-train where the trekkers are making merry in a fashion which emphasises his loneliness and rides off to find Caroline. He does so without too much difficulty and they confess their feelings for each other. Caroline looks extraordinarily lovely as she reclines beside the shimmering waters of a stream, her cheek against his and singing 'More and More', a song attuned to the occasion. There is no hint whatsoever that her person might be dishevelled by the rigours of a harsh and inhospitable terrain. Nor would anyone resent this licence on the part of the film-makers. For Caroline is a visual delight with a circlet of blue flowers girdling her impeccably coiffured hair and a blue dress with a cluster of flowers of matching colour at the breast.

So to the grand finale. When Caroline and Johnny arrive in their wagon and draw rein in a vast square dominated by an imposing ranch-cum-hotel, they find themselves in the midst of a huge crowd of provincials. It is a very colourful farrago which accepts them like old and distinguished friends and they are submerged in a festival of dance and song. Caroline's vocal prowess provides a major contribution as she sings 'Califor-ni-ay', weaving her way through the press. She is conspicuous this time in white and in gold. Braided and bespangled hair and lustrous blue eyes crown this ensemble in a bewitching way.

The flow of melody in the final sequence continues unabated as Caroline, called upon by Johnny to confess to Carstairs her love for another, approaches the gentleman in question at a communal banquet and begs him in a whisper to play the part of a rejected lover. An elderly cowboy, the richest man in California, as kindly perhaps as he is shrewd, responds very charitably although he has never set eyes on Caroline in his life. Alas, a Mrs Carstairs intervenes in some surprise to hear talk of her spouse's infidelity. No sooner has Caroline explained an amusing fiction and mollified a disgruntled Johnny than up rides the cavalry officer claiming her as his fiancee. As a further complication Caroline's father who has been pursuing his daughter all the way from Washington, chooses to arrive at the very moment she is trying once more to convince Johnny that she is not an incorrigible liar and flirt. And thus with suitors introducing themselves as it were from all directions the film comes to a close. Caroline and Johnny are reconciled and they launch into a pot-pourri of enchanting song, she wearing a very lavish gown supplemented by a glittering diamond necklace and scintillating jewels in her hair.

The definitive verdict on 'Can't Help Singing' must be that it is a film which sets you aglow with the utmost pleasure or even warm delight. It is lively always – almost rumbustious in parts and entirely forgivable that some of the characters are as unreal as their activities. One instance in particular springs to mind – the confidence trickster who sells Caroline a wagon which he does not own, who repeats the same trick on her father although the latter is a shrewd politician whom one would not expect to be so bamboozled, and in the final minutes of the film sells the municipal bell, big as a bull, to some luckless peasant. Then there are two crazy individuals with aristocratic pretensions and thick, foreign accents who go charging hither and thither with a stolen trunk through town and wilderness alike. Absurd of course, but their function is typical of the disorientation which at odd moments seems to affect some members of the cast. It is fun decidedly if you are a lover of burlesque. Fortunately Caroline is singularly immune to the antics of others as singlemindedly she treads the road of destiny careless of pitfalls. She is trapped in one of these literally, however, when, obstinately refusing to keep close to her wagon as she is urged to do simply as a precaution on an unknown trail, she plunges into a bog, dainty umbrella and all.

'Can't Help Singing' is not a picture of the Old American West as depicted in hundreds of Cowboy and Indian sagas. With the irrepressible Caroline California bound it becomes a dreamland where there is more harmony than friction, more fellowship than discord, and where Romance permeates the air like a tangible presence, as heady as the scent of jasmine on a summer's eve. Ineffably tender is the scene when Caroline is borne in Johnny's strong arms to a forest's edge whence she wanders abstractedly, then breaks into song whose haunting strains echo afar. The scenery, much of it reminiscent of the plains of Utah where monoliths sprout from a primordial plain like dragons' teeth, is vast as it is magnificent and a fitting backdrop for one whose physical grace and vocal gifts are spell-binding. Indeed, 'Can't Help Singing' unveils so many impressive panoramas whose beauty and serenity and the mysterious tranquillity of wild places remote from the hives of Man is an ideal showpiece for a soloist like Deanna Durbin. And in this film there is the reinforcement of competent singers of diverse range accompanying her in thrilling choruses. This is passion without drama – profound emotion without tragedy – exultant singing in worship of Earth and Heaven and the glories of Nature – in a sense an expression of homage for the bliss of life itself, the privilege of being alive.

There never was a better example of this sense of the ethereal than the moment Caroline emerges from the shade of a green forest into sunlight blazing from a luminous sky, singing 'Any Moment Now', an exquisite melody to rival any operatic aria.

In that scene Deanna is an intermediary between the cinema audience and an indefinable something which I can only describe as the spirit of Everlastingness. And if you should detect any religious significance in that little bit of rhetoric I can only conclude my observations about 'Can't Help Singing' with a fervent 'Amen'.

123

Chapter 17

Lady On a Train

D eanna's sixteenth film 'Lady On A Train', like its immediate
predecessor 'Can't Help Singing', came to the cinema screen in a
year which saw the approaching end of the Second World War and the
defeat of both Germany and Japan, probably, in its aim of self-
aggrandisement, the most deadly alliance of all time in its threat to the
very existence of Mankind. So it is not perhaps an exaggeration to say
that two more Durbin films could only add to the celebrations and
rejoicing of a momentous year which restored peace to the world after
six harrowing years. I like to think that the films featuring Deanna
which were released during that period did much to raise the morale
among English-speaking peoples, civilian and military alike. Speaking
for myself, I always found Deanna's sweet charm and joyous singing an
irresistible combination in any venue, be it as it was at first a cramped
cinema in a blacked-out Britain or a military camp overseas. My
personal reminiscences take me back to a British Aircrew Reception
Centre in Morocco in 1944 and a hanger packed to capacity with
aircraft personnel, those who flew and those who serviced the

Mosquitos and Beaufighters scattered across the tarmac of a busy air base. The film was 'Nice Girl?', borrowed from the local American Headquarters in Casablanca. Such was the enthusiasm it kindled among the British contingent that it was back at their base within a month for a second screening for the benefit of airmen absent on duty at the first showing. Once again the hangar was filled to bursting. And it would be foolish to deny that there were many among a bunch of what Uncle Sam and John Bull would call 'hardened guys' who furtively brushed away a recalcitrant tear or two when Deanna sang 'Beneath The Lights Of Home'. It was a very human reaction on the part of an expatriate audience – yet the film lightened the mood, uplifted many hearts and banished gloomy thoughts about a hazardous tomorrow. As for Deanna herself – thereafter she was the undisputed goddess of the cinema screen to homesick servicemen and I found that to be true wherever I was stationed along Mediterranean shores. Of course it was always an improvised cinema in or out of doors. Shall I ever forget an evening under Algerian skies with a huge African moon glowing grandly above the sacred shrine of the 'Black Virgin On The Hill', the voice of Deanna Durbin ringing through the deeps of the velvet night and a crowd of servicemen sprawled everywhere in all manner of posture listening silent and entranced. Deanna will never know how many or what fantasies she generated in the minds of men far from home who fell instantly in love with a beautiful, talented actress and singer – the archetypal sweetheart too who I doubt not occupied their dreams at the day's end.

In 'Lady On A Train' there are tense moments for our 'blonde' heroine, whose name this time is Nikki, none more so than when we see her flitting through gloomy corridors and cavernous cellars pursued by one whom she believes is intent on murdering her, but eventually running into a psychopath whom she regards as a friend. Mind you, the innocent pursuer is Dan Duryea who featured in, and had the sort of demeanour one associates with Hollywood gangster films, and it might be, carried with him the air of menace beneath his silky exterior which was sedulously cultivated in his more sinister roles. Nikki, a beautiful and cultured socialite with a background of privilege and wealth, is an amateur sleuth and an avid reader of crime stories, especially those involving homicide. And the story unveiled in this rather shadowy film (in the literal sense of the word, for there is an emphasis on dark corners, bare walls and shufflings beyond the candlelight) is fairly complicated, as one contemplating the aforementioned facts might well expect it to be.

Deann Durbin in 'Lady on a Train'
(Reproduced courtesy of Aquarius Library)

The producers of Deanna's films, by the way, acquired the habit of putting her aboard a train in the opening sequences as though it were the most natural thing to do – for example, in 'I'll Be Yours' and notably 'His Butler's Sister'. And trains were involved as early as 'Mad About Music' with its hilarious chase through crowded corridors by exasperated ticket collectors in pursuit of an elusive non-fare-paying passenger – Deanna of course, or Gloria as she was named in the film. As the title suggests, 'Lady On A Train' is faithful to tradition. What follows resurrects another well-tried formula in works of crime fiction. There goes the train, steaming through the night towards New York, then slowing down as it enters the bleak canyons of Harlem. Nikki is curled up on a seat looking extremely pretty and sophisticated but showing only cursory interest in her surroundings as viewed through a plate glass window. The night outside is black but a lighted room with curtains not yet drawn catches her attention. She sees the silhouettes of two men apparently in fierce dispute. One has a crowbar with which he eventually clubs the other to the floor when his victim's back is turned. As the train moves on gradually picking up speed Nikki is convinced that she has been witness to a foul murder. In true detective fashion she tries to work out the train's exact position at the time of the homicide by consulting both a train guard and her wrist watch. Met at her destination by her father's confidential secretary, Nikki manages to get him involved in a dispute over the ownership of a suitcase so that she can steal away and take a taxi to the nearest police precinct. Unfortunately for her, the protectors of public order are sceptical of her assertion that she has seen a murder committed and accordingly a weary sergeant sends her packing when he notices a detective novel in her hand and assumes (not without reason might be the intelligent view) that the alleged crime exists only in her imagination. When she arrives at the hotel accommodation prearranged by her father's secretary, he is just as disparaging as the police about her activities. Indeed, as he pointedly remarks, how could he be expected to take seriously a girl whose detective work in San Francisco for instance had resulted in the arrest of an innocent man who proved to be an FBI agent. The stubborn Nikki, however, is not a lass to be easily dissuaded and she calls at the apartment of her favourite crime author, Wayne Morgan, in the hope that he might be interested in tracking down the villain whom she glimpsed wielding a crowbar. Alas for Nikki's dream of conducting a murder hunt with a celebrated writer of detective fiction. When Wayne refuses to believe her wild story, Nikki goes off alone in search of the bleak warehouse close to a Harlem railway station where she saw the fatal blow struck. A sudden rainstorm leaves her drenched and dishevelled but on leaving the station she catches sight of Wayne entering a taxi with his fiancée and promptly gives chase. Even this simple pursuit (and there is a dual significance here) is given a dramatic touch by Nikki when she hails the driver of a passing taxi and delivers herself of words immemorial perhaps in such a location as the 'Big Apple' – 'Follow that cab'.

The trail leads to a cinema where the peace and quiet of goggling cinemagoers is repeatedly disrupted by Nikki moving up and down the crowded rows of seats in her efforts to reach Wayne and his fiancée. Some patrons are furious at the interruptions but anger is softened somewhat by the witticisms which fly to and fro. It is a scene of disorder which is nevertheless realistic and funny. Those who have known what it is like to have one's view of a cinema screen blocked by latecomers to an auditorium or shall we say people who were born solely to annoy others, forcing their way through to a vacant seat, elbows stuck out and tongues wagging in plea or remonstrance, will have no difficulty in visualising the confusion for which a troublesome though pretty sleuth is responsible in 'Lady On A Train'. Wayne and his fiancée escape hurriedly to rid themselves of their pursuer but Nikki's departure is delayed when a newsreel flashes on the screen showing a picture of a rich financier who has allegedly suffered a fatal accident, for Nikki recognises him as the man she saw murdered in a warehouse. The film continues with impressive views of the mansion on Long Island which was the residence of the dead man.

A thoughtful Nikki leaves the cinema. She is not the least daunted by her failure to find an ally to help her unravel what is now to become a mystery and a conspiracy by evil persons unknown. Off she goes to Long Island.

Next we see her, apparently still full of initiative, but all alone and lonely, a very vulnerable figure, scaling the gates of the Long Island mansion and disturbing two vicious guard-dogs who tear after her and trap her in a pergola. Desperately she climbs high up a trelliswork out of reach of their eager jaws. The dogs bark furiously and make strenuous efforts to dislodge Nikki. Then Arnold (played by Dan

Duryea), a nephew of the murder victim, arrives home. With the help of his chauffeur he brings the hounds to heel. He is a man with a sardonic sense of humour and seems to be mulling all the time over a joke known only to himself.

There are so many developments thereafter that a brief synopsis would not suffice to disentangle them. And to go into intricate details would entail an appraisal of inordinate length. Let me but add that it is at the gloomy mansion that the story and the mystery really starts to unravel. For Nikki is mistaken by Arnold for Margo, a night-club singer and his deceased uncle's lover, or, to use a contemporary term, 'sugar daddy'. Left by chance to her own devices, Nikki blunders into a huge library where the family solicitor is reading the will of the dead financier. Nikki, who has no choice but to pretend to be Margo, learns that she is the main beneficiary. Surprisingly enough the family with the exception of an old aunt does not show much antagonism towards her. And when she drifts from the library after the main portion of the will has been read to search for possible clues to the mystery surrounding an untimely death she discovers evidence in the form of a pair of blood-stained slippers which to her mind is positive proof that the murderer is a member of the bereaved family.

In order to pursue her enquiries Nikki goes to the night-club where Margo works, locks her in her dressing-room and assumes her role as principal entertainer. Oddly none of the staff questions her presence there.

So it is not until the film has run half its course that Nikki sings in public, and a saucy little ditty it is too, titled 'Gimme a little Kiss' with the plea, 'will you, huh?' During the bravura performance she glides from table to table, smiling seductively at fascinated males and paying particular attention to Wayne who is there with his fiancée. Nikki (or rather Deanna) is as enchanting in this musical 'Frisson' as she is in the operatic sphere. One feels that her sophistication is not wholly real – an underlying coyness is there which is in every way disarming.

That sultry, sensual song is in marked contrast with 'Silent Night – Holy Night' which at an earlier point in the film Nikki sings over the telephone to an anxious father in the privacy of her hotel bedroom. On that occasion even an unscrupulous thief waiting in the wings as it were, temporarily forgets his mission to retrieve a bloodstained pair of slippers and seems to drop into reverie as though the music has sounded a chord in his own sinful heart.

The closing sequences of 'Lady On A Train' are action-packed with humans racing and chasing upstairs and downstairs, through dimly-lit alleys and corridors and cellars like crypts which might shelter hideous monsters – fist-fights between Arnold's chauffeur and Nikki's somewhat bewildered ally, Wayne, then between Wayne and the proprietor of the night-club who carried a cat in his arms for most of the time like a devil hugging his familiar. He is a repulsive person at best, a criminal in league with a murderer, and one reflects that his violent end in the night-club, a demise of which Nikki and Wayne are deemed guilty, is not undeserved. The ramifications of the plot become increasingly hectic and necessitate another appearance by Nikki, masquerading as Margo. This time she sings 'Night and Day' in which she gives full rein to human emotion and the octaval splendours we have come to expect of the real-life Deanna.

Remorselessly the story grinds on and we begin to feel that there will be no more singing by our gifted songstress. Nikki finds herself bound for the warehouse where the murder occurred which she saw in the opening shot of the film. Happily, Leslie Charteris, author of the crime story, injects a touch of humour in the closing sequence when Wayne (who more than once in the film is made to seem surprisingly obtuse whenever quick thinking and instant reaction to crisis is called for) puts Nikki in dire peril when he unwittingly disarms the good guy and leaves a murderer to gloat upon several potential victims. But then 'Lady On A Train' is fiction which has more than a touch of fantasy about it – whether it reflects with any veracity the real, conventional world of crime is arguable. But there is no doubt whatever that a blonde Deanna Durbin, though not called upon to display her unique talents as a vocalist to a degree that one would wish (for her voice is so wonderful in its fluidity, in every subtle inflection, in every soaring note) is unquestionably a gifted actress. I must admit that I prefer her role in 'Lady On A Train' to that in 'Christmas Holiday' in which the tempo of tragedy is precise, tortuous and unremitting. For during her Springtime Deanna was a remarkable progenitor of emotional rhythms, of spiritual harmonies which enchant the secret mind and never fail to strike a sympathetic chord in people of imagination and sensitivity who by culture as well as inclination become the beneficiaries of such largesse.

The final scene of the film shows a newly wed Nikki together with her husband on a train steaming through the night, and, it would appear, bound for a honeymoon in some distant, tranquil place. And I wonder how many viewers, masculine gender, watching that train disappear into the darkness were moved to envy the rather egotistical Wayne, albeit he was a creature of fiction. They probably vacated the cinema in a moody frame of mind, conscious of a sense of betrayal perhaps that their screen goddess was pledged to the marital bed and in that allegiance was demonstrating that she's human after all. Yet they would not have doubted that in due time the object of their desire, and perhaps their veneration, would be reborn, hopefully in another fable of Spring, of youth and laughter, of fleecy clouds and azure skies, of innocent, romantic love, and with every trace of malevolence expunged from the script. For to them, uniquely so, Deanna Durbin is a synonym for Light and for Music, and these precious and indefinable abstractions have no place in the cramped cell of Darkness and Despair.

Chapter 18

Because of Him

December 1945, with the shadow of war lifted, saw the arrival of a new film from Universal Studios, i.e. 'Because of Him'. It is impossible not to enthuse over this delightful film in which Deanna Durbin is aided and abetted by two distinguished actors of the cinema screen, both of whom, Franchot Tone in particular, had already starred with her in musicals. In the opening scene comes further promise of rich but droll histrionics from Charles Laughton who was a true disciple of Thespis. He, John Sheridan in the film, has been playing the role of Cyrano de Bergerac for a whole year, during which, to use his own words or an approximation thereof, 'he has died every night nobly and gracefully'. He even removes a false and protuberant nose with the sort of flourish one associates with the cavaliers of a Romantic Age, and then the valedictory curtain falls for the last time upon the scene of his triumph. Then in the dressing-room he is questioned about his next show which is a play entitled 'Strange Laughter'. Both his manager and the playwright involved, Paul Taylor, played by Franchot Tone, put forward the claims of an experienced star of the theatre to become his new leading lady. But Sheridan is non-committal, for the actress the others have in mind is a mature woman and he prefers 'a young actress with the fire of youth'. This voiced preference is the first intimation that that somebody will assuredly be Deanna Durbin in whatever guise she may appear. And so it proves. Deanna is a waitress named Kim Walker who duly makes her entrance in a crowd of theatregoers clamouring outside a stage door for the autograph of John Sheridan. Kim is not among the fortunate ones who obtain the desired signature but she gets a further opportunity some minutes later when she reports for work at a restaurant which is patronised that evening by the celebrated actor himself. Helped by her room-mate and close friend, Nora, she contrives to get Sheridan's signature on a folded sheet of paper blank on the exposed side. A loquacious actor all unwittingly appends his autograph to a letter of commendation on Kim's behalf – which declares among other things (as the two conspirators scan it with unconcealed delight) that Kim 'is a promising young actress who has my warm and sincere endorsement'. (No viewer, I am sure, is shocked by such subterfuge; on the contrary, like me, he probably revels in Kim's duplicity, simply because she is such a joy to watch.) Never was such misrepresentation accomplished so artfully nor with such sweet insouciance. Kim does not flinch overmuch when an irascible restaurant proprietor dismisses her for her poor timekeeping and lack of serious application to her job.

The next morning before making her way to the office of John Sheridan's agent with the letter obtained by false pretences, Kim gives us her first musical offering. The song is 'Lover' and she sings it in accompaniment with her own disc which she has recorded as a form of self-advertisement in her quest for a part in a theatrical production. Kim gives a faultless performance in the manner of one who is confident of her ability. She is as assured that her situation is under control as she is chic in her person.

Action switches to a busy street scene. Pavements swarm with commuters and shoppers, everybody seemingly in a hurry as if to escape Doomsday. Road traffic is massed in noisy, smoke-bound procession weaving down a concrete highway. On her way to see Sheridan's agent, Kim is beautifully dressed, her face aglow with the joy of living, if not the firm expectation of a marked improvement in her fortunes. She is the embodiment of Springtime or so she appears to Paul Taylor, the playwright, who emerges from a flower-shop and follows her on impulse because she looks so captivating. There follows an amusing incident when at a kerbside he pulls her back by the arm and chides her for her inadvertence in not paying attention to traffic signs. Of course there is no danger whatever and Kim can be forgiven for not noticing the 'mythical' car which has put her life at risk, according to Paul Taylor. Comprehension dawns on a mystified girl when he tries to obtain her telephone number and smilingly she sends him packing as it were, assuming quite justifiably that he is one of an urban breed of macho males to whom all femininity is an instant challenge to their egos. There is an element of retributive justice then when he himself with his attention diverted as he watches Kim make off, so nearly ends up beneath the wheels of a passing car.

They are soon to meet again, however, under more formal circumstances, in the agent's office where Kim's credentials, i.e. the bogus letter, have been accepted without question. The agent himself is totally won over by Kim's act as she wanders about his office with such remarks as 'John has told me so much about you', and, still chattering inconsequentially, admires the decor and furnishings, etcetera. In comes Paul Taylor and after his initial surprise at seeing Kim again, he too is impressed by Sheridan's letter until the agent talks of Kim as the actor's new leading lady.

'Not in my play,' quoths he, and declares in a most emphatic way that a tried and experienced actress is required for 'Strange Laughter', not one whose only taste of the theatre has been gleaned in a high-school play. He leaves abruptly, no longer smiling, Kim's charms forgotten, his manner abrasive. But just then a well-known gossip columnist conveniently enters the office and, mindful of the prospect of publicity, the agent tells him that he is going to hold a party in Kim's honour at Sheridan's apartment to celebrate the arrival of a new star in the world of entertainment. Kim is astonished by this development and though apprehensive has no choice save to let destiny take its inevitable course.

The sequence in which we see the promised party in full swing, the radiant Kim the centre of attraction and then the sudden arrival of John Sheridan, driven home from a vacation by atrocious weather, is one brimful of delight and laughter and, if it can be so described, joyous suspense. Kim's utter consternation when the great man enters may well be imagined. The 'Let's get out of here!' from a despairing Nora, ever faithfully at Kim's elbow, is not a practical proposition with all eyes including John's focused in their direction. Neither is escape possible through 'the ground opening and swallowing up' syndrome. The crowd falls apart slowly as John Sheridan approaches Kim, an enterprising lass who now looks utterly forlorn and conspicuously alone. But does she rise to the occasion? Indeed she does! The only stratagem left to her apart from precipitate and humiliating flight is to faint, and it is a swoon she simulates very convincingly as Sheridan moves within a pace or two. So near is he that he has no difficulty whatever in catching Kim in his arms. She is borne away to an elaborately furnished bedroom where a few minutes later, secretly observing Sheridan hovering by the bed with no one else in the room, she passes a hand across her temple, whispering, 'Where am I?' Her whole demeanour is weary and languid as well might be one ostensibly just returned from oblivion. The shrewd Sheridan is fully aware of Kim's pretence. And the subsequent verbal exchanges are fascinating as he pours scorn on her amateurish attempt at fainting. He demonstrates how it should be done – not by throwing the body sideways as Kim did but by sinking gracefully in a heap. However, because of his portly frame even Laughton's professional demonstration reminded me of a porpoise floundering upon its face. After the instruction he brings Kim down to earth with a very direct query – 'Who the hell are you?'

Kim has no alternative save to confess her audacious scheme with the incriminating letter. She has to a certain degree developed some confidence in a famous actor who has been generous enough not to denounce her in front of distinguished guests. She makes clear her ambitions to go on the stage and she is hopeful when he decides to escort her home. They leave his bedroom, he with one arm supporting her, the other holding her right hand at arm's length and her head nestling close to his chest. Then they pose before a battery of cameras and a lively gathering of newspaper reporters. Gallantly Sheridan walks Kim to the front door of the boarding-house where she is lodging with Nora but contrary to her expectations he advises her to go back home to Dakota. Perhaps a more bitter blow to Kim's pride than his rather brusque rejection is his disparaging remarks about acting ability, encapsulated in one biting criticism – 'Good heavens, young woman, you don't even know how to faint properly.'

While a dejected Kim weeps as she makes ready for bed that night, Norah telephones a prominent newspaper editor and informs him of an attempt by Kim to commit suicide because of the way she has been treated by the renowned John Sheridan who has ruined the future she had planned for herself and broken his promises. She makes him sound to the world more like a faithless lover, and for good measure a callous one at that. The press descend on Kim's apartment, followed swiftly by Sheridan who, torn by remorse, lapses into histrionics once more, calling her 'a wounded bird'. He is genuinely concerned about her because he recalls the rather brutal opinion he voiced the previous night and feels responsible for the attempted suicide. Kim receives him like an empress. There is a faraway look in her eyes as she greets him, extending a shapely arm so that he may kiss her hand. 'This mustn't get in the newspapers,' she temporises, while Sheridan takes note of the journal lying on the floor at the foot of her bed. On its front page are banner headlines about his despicable betrayal of an innocent girl.

He soon realises that Kim's dissimulation can mean only one thing – the suicide was fictitious, a ploy to invite the utmost publicity, thereby enhancing her prospects in the theatrical world. He asks, 'Have you ever been spanked, Miss Walker?' Fortunately for Kim he does not put his threat into practice (though I believe his restraint robbed the cinema of a rare spectacle). He can only admire her audacity. Once again Kim and Sheridan walk out of a bedroom in a prescribed embrace to comfort the media with the image of a reconciliation. Sheridan cannot forbear to remark to his lovely companion, 'You and I seem always to be walking out of bedrooms'. And let it be understood that the conduct of both during the scenes therein is above reproach.

Sheridan informs Kim that he intends to take her night-clubbing, which is a means to further publicity advantageous to both. Nevertheless, later when they return to his apartment her lively spirit is once again deflated when he tells her before calling a taxi to take her back to her lodgings that she should contact him again in a year or two. In the meantime she should gain more experience. He sweetens the bitter pill with a kindly observation that 'you are not only a clever little girl, but a nice little girl'. With the lecture over he drifts over to a telephone to call the required taxi but before he can speak into the receiver Kim wanders aimlessly about the room humming the tune 'Danny Boy'. He pauses, then says 'I like that' and urges her to continue. So Kim begins to sing the sad and soulful melody whose haunting sentimentality has enthralled millions across the globe for untold years. So unutterably sweet, so soft and vibrant in turn is her voice, that for once a garrulous actor is smitten into silence. His attitude is almost one of reverence as the pure strains of tuneful song fall in an exquisite deluge upon his ear. How effortlessly, how touchingly, Kim reaches the higher octaves. A single glistening tear oozes down her cheek as she comes to the end of her song, achieving the conventional topnote as a climax and achieving perfect consonance with sound which gradually ebbs away.

There is dead silence in that shadowy chamber until an almost mesmerised John Sheridan eases himself upon a couch and meditates for a moment or two before tossing Kim a copy of the play 'Strange Laughter' saying, 'Catch! Better get to work.'

So ends one of the best and most moving scenes that Deanna Durbin ever enacted upon the screen. It imprints itself upon the memory when much of the other substance of the story might slip into limbo. 'Danny Boy' is always evocative. Yet with Deanna singing it so tenderly and wistfully the melody was not dolorous. The emphasis was not on the grave and the buried dead, rather on the hope of resurrection and reunion – not on the 'roses dying' but a gladsome Spring and transfiguration beyond material life.

In this fashion Kim's initiation into the mechanics of the theatrical art begins. Paul Taylor meanwhile has also convinced himself that his marked hostility to the idea of Kim performing in his play was responsible for her suicide attempt and he visits her flat as contrite as he is conciliatory. But an emotional love scene is abruptly suspended when he picks up her copy of 'Strange Laughter', thus learning of her association with Sheridan and the seeming *fait accompli* with regard to the choice of an actress to star in his show. He accuses Kim of deceit and opportunism and afterwards makes no secret of his opposition to having Kim on the set. He is obstructive in every possible way at rehearsals, even derisive of her acting – and at times inexcusably rude. So uncompromising in fact is he that as the opening night for his play approaches he disowns it and has his name removed from the public advertisements of the premiere. In a last, desperate effort to placate Paul, Kim goes to his hotel but when he opens the door to his suite and she bursts in she finds him still unrelenting.

Did nobody even consider his behaviour altogether irrational? Could he not have trusted the judgement of an experienced campaigner like Sheridan who had no doubt whatever about Kim's suitability for the part she was to play? Or was it just sheer pique at having his wishes ignored?

Kim almost begs him to change his mind but instead he craftily locks her within his room thinking to escape from the hotel while she remains captive. But a security guard and a wondering crowd of hotel guests bears down upon him from all directions. The reason? Having banged upon the door to his apartment in vain, Kim bursts into song – that magnificent aria, Tosti's 'Goodbye'. The thrilling sound of her voice echoes down the corridors without, and bystanders are halted in their tracks by the sheer bliss of that musical expression. Surprised but rapt inmates drift out from their rooms to edge nearer in search of a mysterious soprano. They gather in the passage-way around an embarrassed Paul Taylor. The security guard forces the dismayed playwright to release Kim from his apartment and Kim comes forth still singing rapturously, only to be 'moved on' as the saying goes. Thinking he is free of her Paul hurries to the nearest lift. Once the descent begins there is Kim again, crowding him, looking up tenderly into his face to the enjoyment of others and sweetly bidding him 'Goodbye'. The occasion is humorous enough in essence – a beautiful vocalist giving an impromptu but splendid performance as she pursues a stubborn playwright through the main ballroom and lobby of a grand hotel as far as the revolving front door where he finally eludes her. Personally I would have preferred a magnificent aria to have been sung against a more orthodox background – a vast stage, for instance, an auditorium decked with reds and golds and a concert hall bright with banks of flowers in the proscenium. An impeccably dressed audience too, fallen hopelessly beneath a singer's spell. Tosti's 'Goodbye' is then subjected to constant interruption which I deprecated when I first saw the film and always will, I suppose. Elevators, hotel corridors and crowded lounges do not provide a suitable milieu for glorious melody. And perhaps one could ask nothing more of life when it comes to dying than to take one's leave with that wonderful song ringing in the ear, preferably Deanna's voice with the magic to bestow the ultimate perfection.

The film's ending was perhaps predictable with Kim receiving an ovation after her first live performance in the theatre, and a playwright, belatedly come to his senses, receiving her into his arms. Quite rightly the final shot of 'Because of Him' depicts Kim, supremely happy in the acquisition of both a career and a lover, swamped with floral tributes, and satisfactory enough I suppose as an alternative to a valedictory song which we have come, forgivably, to expect in the closing scene of a Deanna Durbin film. Yet there is virtue as well as wisdom in such repetition since it reminds us that it is not only the warmth of Deanna's personality, an instinctive charm and grace and enviable good looks which endear her to so many, but that voice of liquid silver whose ethos lies in dreams and witchery, which can weave as it were a web of deep emotion long outlasting the individual song. To put it very simply – one cannot envisage the existence of the one without the other.

Deanna's splendid voice is a reflection of a sweet and compassionate spirit, and their affinity is absolute.

Chapter 19

I'll be Yours

Deanna's eighteenth film was 'I'll Be Yours', released in 1947.

It would hardly have escaped notice that in several of her films Deanna played the role of a provincial lass travelling to the big city to carve out a career for herself as an actress, perhaps in musical comedy. 'I'll Be Yours' is one such vehicle. As in 'His Butler's Sister' there is the swift flash of a train New York bound (oh, those wonderful days of steam exemplified by prodigious locomotives driven it seemed by Promethean fire). The monster slows down at an obscure wayside station. We see the legend 'Cobbleskill' (if the eye is not too laggard of course) where presumably Deanna, alias Louise Ginglebusher (a poor example of the art of nomenclature this) begins her journey. She favours a steward with a sudden smile of gratitude when he directs her to a niche in a sleeping compartment which, by implication, she has not reserved. A discerning man that one who, highly susceptible perhaps to the allure of a beautiful young woman, shows his appreciation by offering her a more comfortable facility than a hard and rigid seat in an ordinary railway carriage.

Deanna Durbin and Tom Drake in 'I'll be Yours'
(Reproduced courtesy of The Movie Store Collection)

Louise is obviously not overburdened with cash since on arrival at a bustling terminus she rejects a porter's tentative move to take care of her luggage and, far from hailing a taxi, sets forth on foot towards her destination which is, as later revealed, a cheap and somewhat seedy boarding house conveniently near to theatreland. The thoroughfares are teeming with pedestrians all intent on their purposes, trivial or otherwise. When a fitful wind sweeps away Louise's headgear she seems unaware of the fact until the hat is retrieved by a bearded young man who promptly disappears into the crowd before she can properly thank him for his chivalry. Louise leaves the main artery through a busy precinct and turns into a side-street where there is less turbulence from people and traffic. She enters a small cafe advertising Hungarian goulash at a specially cheap price. The next sequence is one of those fun-filled interludes which make Deanna's films such a treasury of happy memories. None better than William Bendix – waiter-cum-philosopher – whose expositions about the cost of food and the necessary preparations before it becomes a saleable commodity are delivered in a droll but serious manner which makes Louise feel almost ashamed and guilty in that she has quibbled over the cost of a turkey sandwich. And certainly exponential waiters are a new breed in her limited experience of city ways. Seeing that most of the dishes advertised have been taken off the menu by the time of Louise' arrival it is a wonder that at last she is able to obtain a chicken sandwich at a reduced price, thanks to the waiter's generosity. When the young man who salvaged her hat in the street enters the cafe the comedy gathers momentum. Louise watches while he sits down to conduct some legal business with the waiter, both ignoring her while they converse privily. She sees something vaguely familiar about him and then recognises him as the good Samaritan who retrieved her hat. Formal introductions follow between the trio. Louise's surname of Ginglebusher is the cause of a sudden inspiration on the waiter's part. He suggests a future commission for his friend who is a struggling lawyer. And he implies that the aspiring lawyer's impecuniosity is due to his being scrupulously honest down to the smallest detail – and whoever heard of an honest lawyer who became rich? The proposal is that Louise might wish to change her unwieldy family name by deed poll for something less difficult to pronounce, and perhaps less provocative of giggles in those with a ready sense of the ridiculous or facile sense of humour, in which case the young lawyer might take care of the legal formalities. Louise accepts his business card and the little gathering in the café disperses amicably. Louise's next appearance is with a boisterous character who is manager of a large and sumptuous cinema.

His office is more like the boardroom of a Wall Street tycoon. It is learned that he is an old friend of her deceased father and it is for the sake of that friendship that Louise is seeking an opening in the entertainment world which he might well sponsor. All he requires really is a classical dancer for one of his live shows and since Louise admits that she has never had any training in that field all he can do is to offer her a job as an usherette for the time being which she is pleased to accept.

On duty at the cinema Louise meets the waiter again and she returns the consideration he showed her in a dietary affair by conducting him to a seat in the circle instead of the one he paid for, an eagle's nest on the balcony. The acquaintance of an odd pair flourishes and he walks her home. They linger on the steps of her boarding house while they talk frankly of their lives and their ambitions. He is keen to become proprietor of his own restaurant but she has no clear idea of what the future might hold for her as regards a career. Now firm friends, they part in the expectation of meeting again at a social function to be held a few nights later at a fashionable restaurant. The plan is for her to attend this event notwithstanding the lack of an invitation since he is to function as one of the waiters on duty that evening. He will facilitate her admission and ensure that she is well looked after.

And so to the big night and Louise (like the predecessors Deanna played in so many of her roles) enters a spacious ballroom gorgeously clad. She is wearing a frilly black dress with her dark hair beautifully coiffured and the absence of any jewellery gives that touch of simplicity which makes her whole aspect the more striking. One can only guess at the delicate fragrance of her preferred perfume. Feeling a trifle lost amid an animated and garrulous crowd, Louise is relieved to catch sight of her friend as he serves refreshments to the guests, and with exquisite timing, if her intention is to shatter the aura of romance rather than appease her hunger, seizes upon a stick of celery from his tray and munches it unconcernedly. When finally she takes a seat at a side table her chic appearance and ravishing looks, above all her air of dignified abstraction, attract the attention of the industrial baron who is

143

hosting the party. He approaches her table and although he seems to be both elegant and refined, a picture indeed of sartorial perfection, he is dressed in the same fashion as her 'goulash' friend and Louise assumes that he is one of the same species in the employment field. She pretends to be Spanish and is quite dismissive of a very wealthy man until he discloses that he is patron of all the festivities and she realises that he is a person of influence and power. He for his part questions her own credentials and seeing her non-plussed (she can hardly admit to gate-crashing the party) the waiter (played by the wide-eyed William Bendix) intervenes hastily and names Louise as an entertainer. The head of a meat corporation (our old friend Adolphe Menjou in disguise and suave as ever he was), no longer ruffled now that he feels that he has won proper respect for his status from a somewhat disconcerted young lady, is told that Louise is a singer and immediately insists that she should entertain his guests. Louise is reluctant until a sceptical head waiter mutters covertly, 'This had better be good' – the implication being that if things turn out otherwise she will be promptly shown the door, and unceremoniously at that. Louise resents his attitude and agrees straightway to sing, choosing the song 'Granada', a number which gives tremendous scope for an artist with rare talent (like Deanna). The meat baron, the head waiter and Louise's friend especially, look almost stunned as an electrifying soprano voice bursts into life. She moves from the restaurant area which is on a split level down to the main floor and all movement and conversation is suspended by a rapt assembly.

Louise circles the dance floor with deliberate step, adopting that familiar stance of hand on hip as Deanna does when she renders 'Amapola' in 'First Love' and again rendering the 'Russian Medley' in 'His Butler's Sister'. Before the thunderous applause which greets this brilliant debut has drained away, the wealthy magnate seizes Louise by the arm and almost drags her to his apartment upstairs. Nor is she, inexperienced, provincial lass though she might be, left in much doubt as to his amorous intentions. He hardly denies his passion for young girls and gives broad hints that subject to her co-operation in his designs there is nothing beyond her reach, wealth, stardom, etcetera.

When in the distraction of the moment she drops her Spanish accent, he accuses her with feigned seriousness of gate-crashing his party. She is alarmed by his expectation that she will accord him sexual favours in return for his patronage or sponsorship and a profitable career on the stage and when he tries to embrace her she slips hastily out of his grasp and backs away. He chases her literally from corner to corner in a spacious apartment. 'I'm a very rich man,' he pleads, 'I can make you a star.' In despair the hapless Miss Ginglebusher blurts out that she cannot stay any longer – she has to get home to her husband. A would-be plunderer of feminine virtue abandons his pursuit, looking utterly shocked. But, lust mastering his disappointment, he calmly makes the suggestion that Louise should rid herself of her husband and form a liaison with himself. She confides more or less that her spouse is a struggling lawyer and gives the other the 'husband's' business card. Menjou, the meat-man, promises that he will take care of the situation, then Louise can seek a divorce. The consternation of Bendix the waiter, anxious about the fate of Louise at the hands of a known lecher, and his timely intervention with the news that an angry husband is downstairs, brings a hilarious session to a close. Menjou keeps his word and calls on the young lawyer, George Prescott. Only after a lively altercation does honest George, initially suspicious of an unsolicited generosity, agree to enter the employment offered him as a company lawyer in the meat business. Who can blame him for being sceptical about the other's motives and his fear of becoming involved in some crooked financial cover-up which will besmirch his reputation? A man whose office is plastered with such slogans as 'Honesty is the Best Policy' might well be expected to be wary of Greeks – or smooth-talking industrialists – bearing unsought gifts. The 'husband' obstacle surmounted, the meat baron extracts a promised from Louise that she will visit his apartment the following evening. There follows a very enjoyable sequence in which Louise urges George to shave off his beard, saying it makes him look old. George complies with her suggestion and they drive off in his newly acquired automobile, purchased with a cash advance from George's new employer. They go to a lakeside and their hiring of a rowing-boat to join other couples gliding gently to and fro is the prelude to another song from Louise. 'Dreamtime' is the apt title of a number sung slowly and hauntingly by Louise as their boat drifts beneath overhanging branches near the lakeside rim. The foliage dips here and there into the limpid waters.

But the illusion of sublime bliss and serenity is swiftly succeeded by disillusionment, for George anyway. Their return to Louise' lodging is happy enough and their goodnight kiss is a seal on the affection they profess for each other. George even declares his love for her and suggests that she change her name from Ginglebusher to Prescott, his own – which might reasonably be regarded as a devious proposal of marriage. But all is soured from the moment Louise says that she cannot see him the following evening because she has a date with another man. Nor can she give any indication why the meeting with another is necessary. Like an impulsive lover he draws the wrong conclusions. She weeps a little at his going.

In the next scene we are admitted to a boardroom conference at the headquarters of Conrad Nelson, alias Menjou, the wealthy meat baron. An assembly of directors hurries through the minutes of its last meeting and an aimless discussion of future projects, fondly believing it is hoodwinking a young Prescott, newly appointed lawyer to the organisation. As we discover later it is precisely George's shrewdness and intelligent investigation of company affairs which saves Conrad more than a quarter of a million dollars. Louise meanwhile keeps her appointment at Conrad's apartment where to her dismay he promptly extinguishes most of the lights as a preliminary, he undoubtedly hopes, to some amorous foreplay before the main course. But Louise has a further surprise in store for him as he resumes his protracted pursuit round a very spacious atrium. Exasperated by her reluctance to settle into a cosy tête-à-tête, he reminds her that he has fulfilled his undertaking to help her husband in his career. Desperately she tells him that she is not married after all. Simpleton that he is despite his worldliness – he is unaware that she invented a marriage for herself to feud off unwelcome advances, and Conrad's promise to help her 'mythical' husband in a professional way induced her to maintain the fiction.

146

As might have been foreseen, George Prescott, late from the board meeting, arrives at Conrad's apartment to give an account of his stewardship, only to find an angry employer in the throes of indignation at Louise' deception, and far from convinced of the altruistic nature of her intentions in securing sponsorship for the unwitting George. Louise has fled to an inner room to avoid being discovered by George but Conrad summons her forth to resolve the whole situation. A dumbfounded George infers the worst and he leaves brusquely, sure that an unscrupulous young minx has engaged in a sordid affair with an old roue solely to further her ambition.

Conrad realises the truth and Louise' real motivation and becomes the girl's ally, but it takes all his persuasive power to convince George that Louise is wholly innocent of any intrigue. His certainty of reciprocal love at last dissolves all his suspicion and the glad reconciliation is cemented in the final scene of the film in a garden cafe newly opened under the proprietorship of the waiter who first befriended Louise on her arrival in New York. At that inaugural function Louise sings the Sari Waltz almost exultantly while George whirls her round an oval dance-floor. The dance follows a long, loving kiss which is caught in a spotlight probing across the circle of tables and the glittering array of diners. The foaming waters of a cascade as a backdrop to the final embrace of Louise and her partner reflects the indefatigable taste for the spectacular which was part of Hollywood's 'mystique' in the far-off, golden days of its unquestioned supremacy.

Chapter 20

Something in the Wind

Cinemagoers who first watched Deanna's debut in 'Three Smart Girls' in the late Thirties and like myself saw in her an embryonic Venus with a most marvellous voice, could well conjecture that she would grow into a radiant beauty in later life who would be close to perfection. She looks so stunning in the opening shot of her next film, released in 1947, i.e. 'Something In The Wind', that one can feel assured she has reached the peak of her attractiveness and that the promised transition is complete, if not further enhanced by her elegance and irresistible charm. And all these attributes shelter beneath a gentle self-assurance without any lurking sense of vanity.

In this merry musical where pure romanticism is leavened with moments of hurly-burly to which the principal players apply themselves with a will, Deanna assumes the guise of one Mary Collins who is employed as an announcer in a radio programme. Mary is in the habit of signing-off after each transmission with a song from her own repertoire, in this instance the 'Turntable Song'. And she demonstrates that she can swing a tuneful little ditty with the best of the vocalists who specialise in that area. Strangely enough Mary's composed features and a far-away glimmer in her eye as though her thoughts are of unworldly things, seem to me to belie her own enjoyment. Stylishly dressed, stretched out beside the turntable in her stockinged feet and displaying her shapely ankles, she is distractingly attractive. But her skirt is of decorous length and there is no overt hint of sensuality in what otherwise might have been a provocative pose. In a studio marked 'F' she looks almost winsome as she talks into a microphone. Her hair is a mass of dark curls, her make-up impeccable, and she wiggles her toes alluringly in a way no susceptible male could resist. Oh! the contrast between this delightful Circe and the subsequent bathos when Mary's song comes to an end and instantly four fat ladies in an annexe close by burst into some banal chant advertising a commercial product of some kind. Contemporaneously Mary's turntable is occupied by another announcer whose advent brings the wail of police sirens heralding the adventure of an eponymous character known as 'Dynamite Dan'.

The initial impression of a lovely young woman with a charming degree of sophistication superimposed upon, rather than replacing, a natural simplicity, is not undermined by her overall portrayal in the film. If the plot itself is a little far-fetched it does not go perhaps beyond the limits of credulity. And in any case the delectable sight of our Deanna walking, talking, or in repose, or driven to spirited protestation, has put us in a benevolent mood, and all anomalies or improbabilities are forgivable. Yet the proposition that an employee of a busy radio station can be seized in broad daylight and bundled into a taxi cab – to all intents and purposes, kidnapped – whilst two complacent security guards dismiss her shrieks as deriving from some melodrama in process of transmission within the studio, is a circumstance which prepares one for any subsequent inanities. But we must be patient, remembering that what we are viewing is perhaps only the prologue to a musical romance which has yet to sparkle with imagination, ingenuity and wit – remember too that since there are no boundaries to make-believe there can be no grounds for conventional disbelief. The person kidnapped of course is the adorable Mary Collins. Her fault is that she does not take seriously the conviction of certain parties that she is the secret paramour of the head of an organisation known as Read Enterprises, recently deceased, and from whom she has been receiving regular maintenance for an unspecified number of years. The heir to this organisation, Donald Read, meets Mary in the foyer of the studio and wishes her to accept a final cheque to discharge his grandfather's financial obligations and leave him, the grandson, to go ahead with his marriage to a prominent socialite. The inference is that any unwelcome publicity about his grandfather's clandestine love affair will besmirch his family's reputation and jeopardise his own plans for the future. A mystified Mary, who swears she knows nothing at all about an alleged liaison, comments humorously upon the situation and is soundly upbraided by Donald. 'Your levity is ill-timed,' he declares pompously, whereat she declares that she has had enough of such nonsense and turns her back on him. As for Donald, how can he know that his grandfather's former lover is Mary's aunt and namesake with whom the younger Mary lives? We must pretend that the disparity in years between Mary Collins the radio announcer and the departed grandfather, indeed the very feasibility of an intimate personal relationship, warrants no suspicion whatever in the minds of Donald and his grandmother who is under the same misapprehension as himself.

On arrival home after the surprising advent of Donald Read into her life Mary tells her aunt of the strange incident at the studio – an obvious case of mistaken identity she assumes, though she is still angry at the discourtesy she has suffered. But suddenly her aunt, a fragile old lady, begins to drop crockery all over the place while she washes up. She is plainly embarrassed, if not in shock. Then she talks of her past, of her love for Donald's grandfather and why she was unable to marry him. Apparently her status in life was too lowly to fit in with the grandiose ideas of an old and influential family in the upper strata of society. But when young Mary's mother died and her sister, Mary's aunt, adopted a motherless girl child it was the Read allowance which enabled her to support herself and her niece. Young Mary listens sombrely and makes a vow that somehow she will get even with the Read tribe for her aunt's humiliation.

Before the film switches back to the radio station we are given a glimpse or two of the Read family in the palatial home, anxiously discussing the contretemps of Mary Collins and her obduracy. And then suddenly we are introduced once more to dear old Charles Winniger (thrice seen as Judson Craig, father of 'Three Smart Girls') hiding in a capacious chest and eaves-dropping on his relatives. They resent his relationship with the family – he is some nebulous Uncle Charles – and look upon him as a worthless old sponger. His is not an edifying role on this occasion, but he is not the absent-minded duffer we have grown used to in Deanna's earlier films. His existence has a direct bearing on the plot. It is during this interlude among the elite that grandmother voices the bright idea that her grandson should by some means bring Mary Collins to the Read mansion. Although appalled at first, Donald accepts the plan as the only way out of a considerable dilemma. He enlists the help of his cousin, Charlie Read who is in love with Donald's prospective bride, Clarissa, in a venture which entails the kidnapping of Mary Collins at the studio and forcible transfer to the Read family home.

In a beautiful white gown spangled with flowers Mary steps on to the floor of Studio G before a full orchestra. A cascade of silver notes proclaims that she is 'Happy Go Lucky and Free' and her song is for the emissaries from the world of the theatre who are present to determine whether she has the talent to forge a career for herself in New York. No hands on hips on this occasion for Deanna. As Mary Collins she trips to and fro with commendable grace and sinuous motions of her arms. Her coy gestures epitomise a youthful naiveté but there is also a hint of voluptuousness about her performance as though she is contriving, perhaps unconsciously, to weld together two disparate qualities, innocence and sophistication, albeit delicately. Having received the congratulations of the judges on her singing and a promise of sponsorship, she leaves the studio and is swiftly seized by the Read conspirators and whisked away by car. Naturally, civilised folk like the Reads are not contemplating a sudden end to Mary's career by launching her into the same orbit taken by the deceased grandfather. Their hope is that a generous financial settlement will ensure her silence with regard to a patriarch's past indiscretions.

When the hapless Mary Collins, kicking vainly at her captor, is borne into the Read mansion over Donald's shoulder and unceremoniously dumped upon a huge settee, she fairly raves at all and sundry the moment her gag is removed. Stimulating verbal exchanges follow. Donald ignores her denials about any romantic involvement with his grandfather and pompously refers to the spotless reputation of his family in an exclusive society. At all costs there must be no scandal. But naturally all the members of the Read family present want to be fair and propose that she herself should suggest a figure for a final settlement of their obligations. 'I want to be fair', says Mary, seeming to comply with their wishes. Teasingly she mentions the sum of five thousand dollars which they hear almost with stupefaction and exchange swift glances evincing a certain satisfied smugness and relief. Wily Mary senses their reaction and adds carelessly some remark like, 'That'll do for the baby.' The word 'baby' stuns them into a shocked silence. One can almost feel their anguish that there should be a worse entanglement – the existence of a baby, presumably fathered by 'granddad', with a possibility of further demands on the domestic inheritance. Mary rubs salt into the collective wounds when she intimates almost in the same breath that she will settle for a million dollars. Donald is devastated. Grandmother declares to her demoralised brood that 'Mary Collins shall stay right here in this house until the matter is settled'. At least it seems that one member of the Read circle has the fortitude to face up to disaster though it presage financial ruin.

There are invariable twists and turns in the story of 'Something In The Wind' in accord with the prophetic title, one of the most significant being an alliance between Mary and Donald's cousin Charlie to satisfy their individual ends – Mary's to teach the overbearing Read clan a timely lesson for their presumption and Charlie's to win the hand of Clarissa whom he is certain loves him in preference to Donald. The first step in this process is taken immediately when Clarissa pays the family an unexpected visit. Lest Clarissa should get the wrong idea about the presence of another girl in her fiancé's house, Mary has been banished upstairs while the guest is welcomed in the spacious atrium below. The disturbance which follows reminds me of one in 'Three Smart Girls' when Penny makes a fearful racket dragging a bed from one room to another directly above a drawing-room where her father's intended bride was singing. But in 'Something In The Wind' Mary uses a hi-fi to make the most thunderous noise as though a disco was in full blast. A furious Donald is about to investigate when Mary enters the room chattering brightly. She fawns on Donald in such a loving fashion that Clarissa, outraged and feeling humiliated, promptly takes her leave, or in other words, flounces out. An angry Donald rounds on Mary using terms which fall just short of pure invective, the best being 'typhoid Mary'. She, however, is just beginning to enjoy herself, especially when the family lawyer is summoned to make the desired financial arrangements which will safeguard the Read image of absolute moral integrity.

Charles persuades Donald to take Mary out to a fashion show, and this is the prelude to a delightful sequence in which I would say Deanna's talent for light comedy has never been shown to better advantage. Mary and Donald are seated in front of a full orchestra which plays in a subdued way while attractive models file along the catwalk exhibiting the latest creations in the fashion world. The leader of the orchestra who knows that Mary is a prominent radio personality, suggests that she should sing. With a mischievous sparkle in her eyes and eagerly encouraged by Charlie she agrees to perform. What a show and what a tune! 'You wanna keep your baby looking right – dontcher daddy!' Never was coquetry so exquisitely on display. And never was Deanna so saucy and provoking. It is not mere panache to which we are treated – it is sheer ecstasy in movement and sound. Mary is clad in a dark gown awash with sequins and it sheathes her lithe figure in a seductive way. Coyly she props a forefinger under her chin as she makes the round of seated clients of the male gender who either simper or, mindful of watchful partners, contrive to look vacuous. After a while it comes to Donald's turn to receive attention and, noting the presence of Clarissa and her father who have just entered the hall and become more than interested observers, she resumes her song with a will. She leans over Donald from the rear, twirls his hair, loosens his tie and, gliding forward, flings herself on his lap. She strokes his cheek for a moment or two before whipping out his pocket-book, makes pretence of counting the banknotes therein and finally slaps it gently across his face before tossing it nonchalantly against his midriff. A steely-eyed Clarissa stalks out of the salon with her father.

You might well think that Donald's humiliating treatment at Mary's hands would preclude any romantic feeling for his beautiful tormentor. But after Charlie has convinced him that he is using the wrong tactics in reviling his pet hate and advises him to make love to her instead, he follows his cousin's advice and late one evening knocks upon her bedroom door, all conciliatory and perhaps a trifle sheepish. Mary, looking lovely as usual, her coiffeur a dream, her stylish dress emphasising a shapely outline and a very slim waist, is not deceived by his cooing approach, nor responsive to the arm which encircles her as he extinguishes a lamp. When an orchestra conveniently ensconced in the garden outside Mary's suite begins suddenly to play, Mary is convinced of a conspiracy between certain parties. She sings nevertheless in her usual inspirational fashion and Donald for the first time awakes to her charm and unutterably sweet personality. Soulfully he declares his love and she too realises that she can no longer disguise her own feelings for him. She responds to his fervour and his kisses and he for his part will not listen to any confessions she tries to make about her supposed intrigue with his grandfather.

There is not a lot more to tell save that revelations follow in swift succession. The grandmother visits Mary alone and persuades her to believe that she will ruin Donald's career if her association with him continues. Mary leaves the mansion and returns to her own home where she sings a heart-rending melody 'It's Only Love' expressive of the full blight and pathos of frustrated love. She leaves for New York, hopefully to begin a new career on the stage. She is resigned to losing Donald. Then Uncle Charlie (the mischievous Winniger) who is anxious that Mary should accept a large cheque from the Read family so that he can share in the spoils, succeeds in having her arrested on a false charge. (Though the storyteller would have it so, I begin to feel that the spectacle of Deanna in a prison cell so soon after her incarceration in 'Lady On A Train' is becoming a habit on the part of her film producers.)

Of course, in this latest instance, we might well believe that it is necessary specifically to enable her to sing a duet with a prison guard who has an excellent tenor voice of operatic quality. It is indeed strange that so talented a performer should be wasting his time keeping vigil on wrong-doers, parading around with a bunch of keys like a medieval turnkey. Truly the theatrical mind works in wondrous ways! I doubt whether anyone of his diminutive stature would be suited to such an office or even pass a selection board. But it is none the less a fact that in 'Something In The Wind' he is guarding prison cells and his singing in partnership with Mary Collins of 'Miserere' from 'Il Trovatore' is a joy to listen to. A happy incidence has brought two very fine singers together and so the ramifications of the plot become an irrelevance as their tuneful exuberance engulfs the ear. Even while its rapture is still fresh in our minds Mary has received and signed for a cheque for one million dollars from the Read family lawyers renouncing all further claim on the family estate. She leaves the police precinct abruptly as well, as a bewildered and disillusioned Donald arrives belatedly to arrange bail.

All is well, however, for she is soon rehabilitated in his eyes when Mary's aunt calls at the Read mansion to express her contempt for the bigotry and materialism of the inmates and to return the cheque. The gesture is conclusive proof in their minds of young Mary's honesty and sincerity and they realise how foolish was their mistrust of her. Mary and Donald are brought together in the film's final sequence when she is to make her debut on television as a singer. After some buffoonery on the part of Charles the cousin (a trademark of Donald O'Connor who plays the role) Mary comes on stage to give us a reprise of 'Happy-Go-Lucky and Free' whilst in the wings sits the smiling Read family, fully prepared to accept Mary into its tenacious fold. Never mind – forget the fatuity of human values and human presumption – Donald is close at hand, love shining in his eyes and his thoughts on blissful days in store with the adorable Mary. Let me but add that for me 'Something In The Wind' is another example of the fine quality of Deanna's acting which never truly received the accolade it deserves. She showed herself to be a supremely talented artist in an infinite variety of situations compounded of comedy and drama, laughter and tears, excruciating fun and deep emotion. There is no better proof of this than in the role she played in this film as well as the serious performance in 'Christmas Holiday'. What could be more diverse than these two parts? They called for a complete change of character – from the mournful mood of the latter film to the mercurial in 'Something In The Wind' – from poignant sensitivity to gay abandon. As for the vocal element in the expressive form of sweet melody, as Mary Collins Deanna demonstrates her mastery of the operatic art as much as her inspired rendering of popular songs or less stylised musical material. Her genius lies in her gift of melting our hearts the one moment with an old-fashioned tune of simple sentimentality and switching smoothly next to a classic formula which may well be an aural experience to lift you in your seat.

Chapter 21

Up in Central Park

'Up In Central Park', Deanna's penultimate appearance in a major film, has through the years, beginning with film critics in May 1948 when it was first issued, attracted a lot of adverse comment from sour pens which seemed to have been dipped in vitriol before being committed to paper. But I reflect that so-called experts in that particular field of appraisal are forever looking for perfection and whining when they consider the finished product falls short of their expectations. But perfection in itself is an elusive concept; and it does not become true of anything by the consensus of an informed coterie, a self-styled elite whose enlightenment is at best amorphous, bearing in mind the fallibility of all human pretension. Its judgements are often governed by cynicism or individual preference born either of arrogance or pique towards society at large and its predispositions. That said, I must confess that I did not find 'Up In Central Park' as enjoyable as most of Deanna's films, in particular the cinematic revels which came in swift succession in the years 1936 – 1941. Deanna is essentially a songstress to exalt the spirit and detach one from the workaday world. Much as we admire and love her for her unpretentious good looks and sweet personality – deeply though we are moved by her warm and compassionate nature – it is her marvellous voice which is the quintessence of the living being. And in this last but one film she made in Hollywood she is rarely given the opportunity of demonstrating its power and range for our enjoyment and delight. Two unremarkable songs and a snatch of opera is all that is on offer in that vital field, which inclines one to the view that the film director, whatever his reputation at the time, was for once incredibly foolish in his failure to exploit Deanna's unique talent. I can only suggest that such a musical injection would have improved the film immeasurably and for me revived interest in a story which at times flagged miserably, concentrating more on political chicanery and the sordid ambitions of corrupt officials than the future of an Irish immigrant girl. For such was Deanna's humble status in this confused affair of parochial intrigue and a crooked boss manipulating franchise to his material advantage.

Once again (as in 'The Amazing Mrs Holliday') a film opens with a ship from overseas arriving in the United States with a large quota of immigrants from overseas. Rosie (Deanna) Moore and her father, Timothy (was it pure chance that dad was given the same Christian name as a ship's bosun in the earlier film?), seeking admission to a land of opportunity although on this occasion the port of destination is New York and there is no retinue of orphan children.

Once again Deanna has to forego the sartorial finery which suits her so well for the practical and inelegant dress of the peasant class. Rosie treats her fellow passengers to a lively song 'Say Can You See' while skipping agilely about a crowded boat deck. Then all too swiftly she is submerged in a throng of hopeful aliens all rather awed by the expansive vistas unfolding before it – America, brash, noisy, vast, strange and vibrant beyond imagining. Rosie and her father are told of voting in progress for the election of a new town mayor and are urged to vote for one named Oakley, in reality a puppet of an infamous character known as Boss Tweed who is wont to bribe (or threaten, if that is expedient to discourage rivalry from others, including reformers) anyone who may be of use to him in the furtherance of his disreputable ambitions. Rosie's ignorant father, naively accepting at face value the hearsay about Tweed's altruism and philanthropy, votes no fewer than twenty-three times under many aliases for Tweed's nominee. With so many crooked influences at work, Tweed succeeds in his objectives, but while he is celebrating at his headquarters he and his cronies become aware of a girl who is apparently stirring from sleep on a settee in his spacious atrium. It is the intoxicating Rosie who, weary after long voyaging and perambulating amid a crowd of local townsfolk, has inadvertently wandered upstairs into Tweed's private apartment and fallen into a profound slumber. But she is quite innocent of eavesdropping on their privy conversations, as they discover after some questioning; and when Tweed learns from her lips that he owes much to her father for his multiple voting he waxes enthusiastic about the Moore family. He sends for Timothy and engages him as superintendent of Central Park at an inflated salary, seeing him more as a useful sycophant than someone whose goodwill is essential to his plans.

Incidentally, the role of Boss Tweed is played by Vincent Price, a most surprising choice, like inviting Dracula to a tiny tots' tea-party. One might say nevertheless that he does his best with an unsympathetic role – and it is to his credit that he shows a forbearance when finally brought to book which he seldom exhibited in his more sinister roles of evil wizard, mad inventor or crazed psychopath. That Rosie arouses sexual desire in him can be taken for granted, and one of the funniest scenes in the film results from his invitation to Rosie to dine with him. A table is spotlessly arrayed – flowers, wine, soft lights, subdued music – all the prerequisites for torrid love-making are in place. But Rosie's father Timothy is more worldly wise than Tweed has given him credit for and makes a timely arrival to interrupt what might have proved a trying *tête-à-tête* for his daughter. Surprising but admirable is the bonhomie shown by a frustrated suitor (which you might guess is a euphemistic term for 'lecher').

Though Rosie obstinately maintains her friendship with Boss Tweed whose integrity she refuses to doubt, the real interest is provided by a reporter with the *New York Times* who, suspecting

Tweed of malpractices, is eager to expose him for the unprincipled wretch that he is. He finds an ally in Timothy who was previously loyal to his boss. But the old man's eyes are opened to the other's villainy when he acquires enough English to read for himself and to understand the fulminations of a reformist press against a political opportunist and trickster. An alliance between the reporter and Timothy results in their making a forced entry into the office of the newly elected mayor in search of incriminating evidence that will put an end to Tweed's dominance in local government and expose him as a cynical fraud. A mayor on the verge of drunkenness after an evening's carousal returns unexpectedly to interrupt the intruders, but moved by their insinuations that Tweed regards him with contempt as one incapable of exercising real authority, he tells the full story about Tweed's fraudulent organisation. Written records are made available to the *New York Times* which makes them public under banner headlines.

The exposure of Tweed as a crook and fraudster is made in a dramatic way. He and a privileged company with Rosie as guest of honour are celebrating at a party and Tweed romantically drinks champagne from Rosie's shoe as a token of his deep affection for her. Laughter and merriment is unrestrained until one of Tweed's henchmen enters the room waving a newspaper giving fully authenticated details of the master's dishonest business affairs. One by one his cronies take their furtive leave until Tweed is left alone with Rosie. Poor, disillusioned, little Irish girl! Yet she does not reproach him. She is so numbed by the revelation whose truth she has long suspected but which she refused to believe. It means the end of both her friendship with Tweed and the operatic career he has promised her. She goes forth under the stars where Nature holds quiet sway and only the whisperings of descending night assail the consciousness and the soft folds of darkness are a salve to distress. Thither to soothe her despair comes the reporter who has won Rosie's heart despite her initial distrust of his stance as a moral crusader, and devoted daddy Timothy. The trio turn their backs on the audience and walk away, symbolising a farewell which is somehow wreathed with gloom. I feel that the political intrigue which was the film's main theme, the machinations of the powerful and the plight of the oppressed, have been paraded in an unreal and superficial way. There is little of the widespread brouhaha one might have expected of scandal in a great metropolis like New York – no grand drama commensurate with the exploitation of the masses by the mighty. Even the denouement with Tweed facing ruin is subdued – no sign of outraged citizens clamouring at his portal. On the other hand the principal player in this lukewarm odyssey is restricted to one sprightly song on an immigrant ship and much later 'Carousel In The Park' a tuneful vintage number but no challenge to Deanna's vocal range. The classical excerpt which is not completed, is hardly memorable when one ponders on the glorious arias of her previous films, all sung in a fashion which thrilled the senses and set the spirit soaring in an apotheosis of the vocal art. There must have been ample material available to script-writers and producers alike to have made 'Up In Central Park' a classic of the film industry even as, I am sure, there were perspectives in Central Park contemporary with that age whose existence we would never suspect from the mere glimpse or two we were given of a celebrated amenity – a green arena through which a vast metropolis drew breath. And Deanna in the person of Rosie was almost shamefully neglected in respect of a legendary talent on which fewer and fewer demands were made in the later stages of her Hollywood career. Looking back on those years the paucity, and it well may be the inadequacy, of scripts presented to one of Deanna's acting ability, apart from her singing which would have ensured triumph for any major musical, is as inexplicable as it is sad and lamentable. One can only speculate on the joyous, heart-warming films which might have been made, the scores of melodies classical and traditional, and simple but lovely songs which Deanna has sung perhaps only in the privacy of her own home with her family around her. In the sense that by such restriction the world – at least the world of those who appreciate superlative singing – has been deprived of the matchless ministrations of a great artist – I can only bemoan the loss. And we who have known no pleasure to equal that of listening enraptured while Deanna sings must take comfort in the films and recordings that yet remain.

Chapter 2 2

―――― ⌒꒱⌒ ――――

For the Love of Mary

In the film 'For The Love Of Mary' which came to the cinema screen in September 1948 and was the last one made by Deanna for Universal Studios, she is not always the sweet-tempered little girl of her earlier films. Gone is the shy air of the girl from the deep country looking so unsure of herself. Much less evident too is the nervousness or timidity which made her seem the more endearing in masculine eyes and never failed to arouse the chivalric instincts of those who are the non-canonised Georges of today.

In this light-hearted affair, more nonsensical than serious, she is a supremely confident and sophisticated young lady who mingles with great personalities in the highest echelons of government and legislature, and far from being overawed by such contacts, positively revels in the association. Her self-assurance and tact in delicate situations excites their admiration and wins their warm approval. As the film nears its end she becomes a key element in vital deliberations involving national security.

Deanna's skill as an actress in a somewhat complex role never flags and you feel that there is more natural inspiration about it than mere theatricality. I do not believe it was ever her desire to be intellectually stimulating, not consciously anyway. All her films, thanks

162

to her persuasions, were prolific in generating the emotions which are good for the human spirit and soften the miseries of everyday life. And thankfully, even stories which lacked cohesion were buttressed by the heartfelt, stirring songs which her more enlightened producers made part of her repertoire.

'For The Love Of Mary', despite an unwieldy plot, gives Deanna the opportunity of recording four songs of contrasting sentiment, two of them classical in concept. And a reprise or two of the sentimental numbers might have provided some further compensation for passivity elsewhere in the script. Although this musical, if that is not an extravagant way to describe it, did not overflow with lilting melody as in 'Spring Parade', there is one sequence in a restaurant run by an amiable friend of Mary Peppertree (which is Deanna's pseudonym in the film) in which she sings a Viennese Waltz song while serving dishes to distinguished executives and judges of the High court, and withal smiling throughout in a way which moves you to dreamy distraction. She does so mysteriously and half-mischievously. Never has she sung so delectably. 'I'm cheerful, ever cheerful,' she trills – and 'My heart is flying high on the wings of a song' – beautiful stanzas, unforgettable rhythms set to inspired music – mellifluous notes which enchant the attentive throng. This is followed some time later by a homely sing-song with accordion and piano accompaniment in which Deanna gives a restrained but tuneful rendering of old favourites like 'Moonlight Bay' and 'Kathleen'. Such haunting and nostalgic melodies, you feel, should be but the precursors of others of matching sentiment and to continue *ad infinitum* until the entire repertoire of the lovely singer has been drained and you are helplessly adrift in some infinitude where existence is unreal and only the dream lingers. In connection with this musical soirée I remember in particular an old man sitting by the piano while Deanna sang. He played an accordion almost absently. There was a faraway look in his eyes so brimful of reflection and tender memories, perhaps of his younger days. It left you in no doubt of the imagery woven by Deanna's voice. Deanna's final rendition in the film was 'Largo Al Factotum' from the Barber of Seville, a surprising choice more usually interpreted by the tenor rather than the soprano. But even so I have never heard that ebullient aria sung more vibrantly or with such panache. She even dons a moustache to further the illusion. Her performance is a positive delight and it was unkind of her director to require her to take a step backward on the climax of her aria with her arm raised in dramatic gesture, only to tumble forlornly into the dark waters of a lake.

The plot of 'For The Love Of Mary' is scarcely credible – in fact the tale unfolded is farcical or at least one not to be taken too seriously. Look at it as simply a vehicle for Deanna to entertain her vast public and one will not cavil at all at the fact that it is neither a musical nor serious drama in the strictest sense. Deanna as Mary Peppertree (even the name is an absurd amalgam) is a switchboard operator who transfers from the judicature to the White House, specifically it seems so that she may become involved both with the President himself and a persistent young man named Paxton who is seeking an interview with the Head of State in order to point out that an island where a U.S. naval base has been established is his rightful property. But this primary reason for his stubbornness in making repeated telephone calls is veiled almost to the end of the film. In fact, though he is a marine biologist, he leads Mary to believe that his sole interest is in fish, albeit she is vague about the actual significance of that obsession. An underlying theme is the lively interest the President develops in Mary's welfare, an interest which has its origin in a series of telephone conversations between him and Mary. She discovers that he is suffering from a cold and she offers a remedy while he for his part hears her hiccoughing at the other end of the line (a habit of hers whenever she is anxious for some reason) and advises her to breathe deeply into a paper bag. Moreover when inadvertently she leaves his personal line unplugged he overhears details of her tangled love life, in particular of a lawyer and a prospective suitor whom she does not wish to marry despite the fact that her father, a security guard at the White House, approves of him as a future son-in-law. A benign President who incidentally never makes an actual appearance in the film instructs his own nominee, a naval lieutenant, to escort Mary to a party which she is due to attend. But Paxton as well as the lawyer becomes involved in these capers so that Mary Peppertree ultimately finds herself surrounded by three strapping young admirers clamouring for her favours.

Deanna Durbin in 'For the Love of Mary'.
(Reproduced courtesy of The Movie Store Collection)

(I can only comment that it was extremely gratifying for once to find Deanna being fought over by potential lovers. In so many of her films she had to play the role of a girl obliged to do the chasing, a trend which began in 'That Certain Age' and continued in 'Nice Girl?'. It was refreshing to hear a certain naval lieutenant proposing marriage within hours of their first meeting. What a contrast with Robert Cummings in 'It Started With Eve' who was so tardy in acknowledging the pretty and adorable Anne whose charm and sweetness rejuvenated an old man teetering on the grave's edge!)

Ultimately Mary is the intermediary between White House authorities and a complacent biologist who owns a piece of real estate appropriated by the military in ignorance of its rightful ownership. Paxton turns out to be the chosen one to share Mary's life. But my own feeling is that her future days would have been more exciting in the arms of the naval lieutenant who is sent off on a commission far from home so that he might never again cross Mary's path. He had the same calculating but saucy glint in his eye and the same look of adoration on his face when as young Tom Holliday he wooed and won the mission girl from China in 'The Amazing Mrs Holliday'. And by some coincidence he was also a nautical man in that production.

A frivolous cinematographic outing then is 'For The Love Of Mary' in which Deanna coped easily with none too strenuous demands made upon her talents as both actress and singer. But what a pity her producers and sponsors of those far-off days of the Forties did not feature her in a major musical in Technicolor with an able or even distinguished cast and with Stokowski perhaps as the principal maestro in the show conducting his so very accomplished orchestra. With a gifted vocalist in the lead role in a fiesta of song and dance and excerpts from the great composers to add magic as well as supplement modern lyricism and musical composition, it might well have been a production in the world of melody (like Romeo and Juliet in the sphere of classic drama) to linger enduringly in memory and provide a legacy of exquisite pleasure for generations unborn.

Deanna Durbin showed time and again what a superb singer she was in the fullness of her youth. We can only surmise what heights of excellence she might have reached in a professional career of considerably longer duration than the single decade or so when she was the darling of the cinema screen with a world-wide appeal, when her name was evocative of Springtime, of joy and romance and song as divine as it might ever be in the thinking of mortals. And if this lengthy review of her films has been more encomium than dispassionate appraisal, never was such tribute more richly deserved.

Chapter 23

———— ⌒᚛᚜⌒ ————

Detailed Appraisal
of Deanna

I once read an article by a critic in the world of opera in which he described the music he had heard as 'luxuriant'. It related specifically of course to a soprano and her singing. But to me the term seemed an odd one for an experienced writer, and one presumably selective in his phraseology, to use in respect of something whose expression in a supreme form in the individual is a divine gift and to Mankind in general an immeasurable bounty. In its purest guise music can give such a degree of pleasure that the sound itself may become almost an abstraction – the mind, shorn of volition, floats unaccountably away in a cloud of ecstasy. Luxuriant? Never! For music is of a texture which is indefinable. Inspired, it can best be described as an ennobling influence, kindling both exaltation and wonder. It has the merit, if not the virtue, of purifying the soul.

Nobody in my view has ever been more articulate in the language of music than Deanna Durbin. But I would never use the term 'luxuriant' in respect of her singing. For that was endowed with the kind of spirituality which was the basis of all the reactions set forth in this book as an illustration of music interpreted in an inimitable and superlative way.

Deanna's singing was inimitable because it was so glorious. At a certain level of expression, shall we say halfway between her lowest octave and her thrilling top notes, there was always a thrilling intonation, warm and slightly tremulous, which was unmistakably Deanna's. Hearing the singing with the singer screened from view, still I would have no difficulty in identifying the source. It was as if a fire, though brightly burning, became suddenly suffused with a rich, golden incandescence. Yet there was an underlying restraint particularly evident when she sang refrains which were nostalgic, of times mourned, of loved ones lost and love unrequited. I was never aware when she was singing, of the unrelieved crescendo which is often a conspicuous fault in vocalists today who with no sense of mood or modulation just 'belt out' their songs, and what is worse, with distended jaws and eyes staring with the physical effort of expelling intolerable sound, not to mention the 'gargoyle' effect upon facial muscles agonised by exertion. They remind me more of the costermonger proclaiming his wares than disciples of Euterpe. Deanna's voice on the other hand was always superbly controlled – its mellifluousness flowed like a pristine tide into the depths of one's consciousness. And as a visual indication of a gifted and trained singer, when she reached and sustained an exceptionally high note there was never any distortion of her features. Often she was smiling simply and tenderly as though she herself were detached from the source of melody.

And talking of music critics I would venture to suggest that there are many among them today of no great age who have never even heard a Deanna Durbin recording or watched one of the films which were enlivened and enriched by her songs. I would like to believe that if such pleasure ever came their way the experience would be something of a revelation introducing them to a new dimension in the vocal art whose effect might well induce them to revise the criteria by which they judge the performance of singers, great or not so great.

Whether or not such critics would become devotees of a singularly talented artist of an earlier generation I cannot tell. But for my own part it is my good fortune to be able to reminisce warmly, even interminably, about halcyon days of long ago when Deanna was empress of Hollywood and people from every strata of society flocked to the cinema to hear her sing. They sat in hushed rows wrapped in a cocoon of sweet content, enthralled by visual wonders and the 'inimitable' sound of Deanna Durbin's voice flowing from a silver screen to unleash invisible threads of enchantment upon willing captives in the darkened reaches of the auditorium. Whatever the time of the year, the romantic tales in which Deanna cast a magic spell perpetuated in the mind the illusion of a lasting Spring. There could never be cold or gloom or stark despairs with Deanna singing to the world, rendering for the universal pleasure her sparkling tunes and dreamy melodies – her tender arias – her lively, uncomplicated waltzes – sometimes seductively soft in the modulation of her voice, at others ringing exultantly with true, operatic resonance as the notes soared in breathtaking sequence. Subdued in cadence or hushed with nostalgia and sudden wisp of reverie, tearfully sentimental or uplifted in an ecstatic burst of sound, that matchless soprano voice reached into the very heart, ruling all perception, imparting a sense of undiluted pleasure, obliterating all else. One could feel that in the darkness of the theatre watching eyes were aglow and lips were hushed. It was no wonder that Deanna was, as she is still, idolised so very much. She thrilled millions with her varied repertoire. I must be visionary and say that it was emblematic of the joy which has the nuance of the everlasting, shades of sorrow muted by optimism, the desires and the dreams, the hopes fulfilled or frustrated, which are the mainsprings of all emotion.

When Deanna sang the songs of yesteryear as well as the beloved arias of classical composers she melted the human heart, though that may be a trite phrase to use in a lofty context. Of all singers who ever sang in public hers was the voice which was unmistakable as much for its effortless rhythm and subtle power as its ineffable sweetness of tone. It was like a priceless gem with numberless facets, symbolic of the wonder of life and the wonder of being alive. It was a voice which, whatever the melody or the words it intoned, kindled fancies of Springtime and of burgeoning blossom, thoughts of perpetual regeneration to soften the dread of life's impermanence. In its timbre as in all its cadences there was no traceable rhythm of despair, no sorrow at the transience of things but a sense of thanksgiving for the blessings that are. It evoked emotion to make the heart throb even as it bequeathed memories to soften the meditations of days unborn. In an indefinable way it sparked images to which the mind gives sharper definition than the seeing eye, a nebulous realm where sound and vision are interwoven and where one knows instinctively that every tender dream of love comes to fruition.

To my mind Deanna Durbin made all the singing of her contemporaries seem drear and ordinary. The darkened cinema halls of a bygone age were illumined by her bright halo. Her appeal then, and still treasured by those of us who can never forget the rapture of those days, was timeless, and assures her of an unassailable place in the history of the cinema. She remains the indestructible image of perfect naturalness, of youthful charm and innocence. Artlessness so rare as to invite admiration and wonder instead of studied speculation was part of her charm; and her marvellous, often bubbling sense of humour augmented the magic of her endearing personality. Personally I never confuse the simple unaffected country girl of 'Spring Parade', reprimanding her goat, haggling like a housewife of frugal ways over the price of some commodity, with the carefree but mischievous young woman who sings, 'Gimme a little kiss, wontcher, huh?' in 'Lady On A Train'. Though the roles were disparate she was still the same loveable Deanna. Her success in films did not spoil her in any way. To me it seemed her nature remained always warm and companionable. She had the gift of humanity in her approach to life. Her capacity for kindness, for love, for quick sympathy and understanding, was never breached by the kind of wanton ambition which tramples upon and scorns the needs and susceptibilities of others. And I'll wager that during the years of her well merited fame she was as much the darling of the very old as the child still to grapple with the marvels and mysteries of Creation. And what better tutelage for the young at a tender age than the sight of Deanna and the thrill of her song!

I can only lament the fact that her working life at Universal Studios was of such brief duration. In roughly eleven years she starred in films which have delighted and fascinated generations of men and women who have an ear for sweet harmony and true melody, whose taste is for something more edifying than the dreary music which is the vogue today. Being somewhat old in years and mindful of a past age when, as Deanna might say, 'mothers taught their children how to sing' I cannot understand why music critics today write so fulsomely about pop artists and certain popular vocalists who are more energetic than tuneful, and in respect of those whom I would call the romantic icons of a decadent age, use such terms as 'awesome talent', 'fabulous entertainer' etcetera. Should I wonder whether I am missing something? Are they privy to a secret I am unable to share? The fact that some of these performers, who either croon unintelligibly into a microphone or engage in vocal pyrotechnics, are paid incredible sums of money for their efforts, or should I say, physical gyrations, and that many are greeted wherever they go by hordes of untidy fanatics, some weeping with hysteria or fainting from fatigue resulting from bizarre hero-worship, does not lessen my conviction that their talent, such as it is, must be the creation of publicists whose musical world is a cultural vacuum. They talk of genius when I can sense only mediocrity. Electronic gadgetry which is so widely used by the pop fraternity today, to my mind serves only to amplify sound which in the lowest key is unremarkable and at full blast inflicts excruciating torment on the ear. I can only hope, as will those who share my preference, that the new cult is but a transient one. The followers of that cult are bourgeoisie in the kingdom of music where the aristocracy are the exemplars of the true art – the creation of sounds which are infinitely sweet and harmonious.

If singing itself is a form of art, to be assessed perhaps more by its effect than its exercise, it could be said that I am being too forthright in my criticisms of pop music or any cacophonous equivalent. And it may be that for millions it has a fascination as deep-rooted as my own for the sweet and beguiling harmony which is best enjoyed in a quiet setting free from any turmoil near or far.

Art it is true has a myriad faces.

Though not wishing to be accused of obliquity, I must simply reflect the hope that the future may bring renewal of a desire in the hordes who seem so lacking in appreciation of music which is really melodious, for the kind of singing in which Deanna Durbin excelled. I hope furthermore there may one day come another (dare I say others) such as she to add enchantment to life and a quickening to jaded ears which have not heard the message of sweet harmony.

What else needs to be said about 'Deanna of the Golden Voice' than whom none was more deserving of our adulation as well as our gratitude for the joy and pleasure she brought into countless lives. A pen such as mine cannot but be discursive in the urge, if not the need, to amplify even at the risk of repetition what has already been written.

From the very first year of her appearance on the screen I do not think that those who supervised her career ever called upon her to overtax a voice which still had to mature. I can only presume that she accepted uncomplainingly all the groundwork and tiring impositions, tedious though they might have been, but which were necessary for the transition of a youthful singer of great potential into a cultured soprano of unrivalled excellence. That merely an enviable proficiency would not have suited Deanna's aspirations is manifest in the superlative quality of the singing itself, something which is surely only acquired by years of training and dedication to an ideal.

When Deanna turned her back on the film world she left behind a glorious memory that has never dimmed after nearly half a century. Her films will always remain a treasure chest to be opened on occasion for the pleasure of those who will never entertain the thought of an ageing film-star. Deanna will always remain unique in her coming into the light and her sudden disappearance, in some ways a creature of fantasy but conventionally a beautiful young girl who grew into an even lovelier young woman and will stay perennially young. For that is the way it is and the way we would have it, we who will ever be her loyal subjects *in absentia*. As with the woman, so with that unbelievably gifted voice of hers whose richness of sound was sweet balm to the spirit and a spur to the imaginative mind. She will never be a nebulous image from a past age but a shining star in the firmament of memory. Nowadays when the current vogue regrettably is for vocal discord and the blare from electronic circuits flails the consciousness with repetitive rhythms and vibrations, Deanna's voice is a whole orchestra in itself – its interpretation forever cultured and tuneful – its every note a message of perfect bliss to the listening ear. Though the sweetest sound in its insubstantiality may be swift to fade, there is nothing more real or pervasive than the memory of it which lasts as long as life itself.

It occurs to me here that it was extremely fortunate that Deanna never got into 'heavy opera', the turgid dramas which call invariably for full-throated bursts of song, sometimes entailing the principal characters, tenor and soprano, vying as it were with each other to produce the greater volume of sound. In so many operatic extravaganzas there are histrionics painful to watch, a plethora of dramatic gesture and the bedlam of conflicting vocal chords which is in no sense musical. It might be called classic opera but strangely I find it as much a trial to give ear to as the screeching from the pop world. Thank heaven that in all her films Deanna concentrated on singing that one listened to with rapture, the perfect sense of bliss – melodies which are incredibly sweet and make dreamers of us all. Every song that Deanna sang was an artistic adventure and only once in all her films was I disappointed when she burst into song. That was in 'Up In Central Park' when she was singing some – to me 'obscure' – operatic excerpt in the presence of an unscrupulous politician who was her sponsor and would-be lover and an impresario who had been recruited to further her career.

It is reasonable I suppose to assume that even the most gifted songstress can occasionally sing below par as it were or sound perhaps a little discordant to the untutored ear. But I never for once doubted that in all her films Deanna sang in perfect control of her voice. Furthermore, only when the occasion demanded could one detect the kind of tremor expressing the deep feeling of a person under mental or spiritual strain. It is no secret that the muscles controlling the vocal chords respond more readily to stress than others, making the voice quaver, and a singer so affected is often unable to sustain the note or even to sing in tune.

I remember two situations in particular when Deanna was called upon to sing in an emotional situation – the moving melody 'Home Sweet Home' in 'First Love' and 'Goin' Home' in 'It Started With Eve'. And how delicately she performed! First a sob bringing an abrupt end to the song in question. She demonstrated to perfection the 'break' in the voice which comes of wretchedness of spirit or foreboding about the prospect of a miserable future.

If at this point I subscribe to the view that it was Deanna's incomparable voice and her talents as an actress which were the factors winning for her the admiration and affection of audiences world-wide, it is not to deny that there were other considerations contributing to that appeal. The youthful and wholesome freshness which draped her being like a cloak of light, an effervescent personality which did not disguise swift sympathy for others, were qualities that seldom failed to invite a warm response as readily from strangers as those who knew her well. But I would also refer to her more than merely attractive physical charms. Deanna was undoubtedly beautiful, though in her films she never showed herself guilty of conceit in this respect. Not a hint does she give that she might be thought exceptionally good-looking. Indeed, if I may put it so, she lacked the fault of affectation.

It has been written that this wonderful girl whom I have always thought of as a prodigy never to be forgotten rather than one who enjoyed a temporary stardom, was neither glamorous nor particularly beautiful. My comment must be – never was there such erroneous judgement. What, may I ask, is beauty in a girl or young woman? Something startling and pleasing to look upon? Something which kindles admiration, and in the masculine mind desire or even lust? Yet beauty in its truest manifestation does not lie wholly in the lineaments of the face, however perfect their configuration. Deanna's features when she was simply composed or dispassionate might have seemed tranquilly attractive, but what a transformation when her face broke into a smile! What a bright, intrinsic glow was then unleashed like a flower unfolding its petals to the sun! In her jolly or mischievous mood the effect was the same. It made one feel privileged, even exalted, to bathe in its radiance. What a mirror of spiritual expression lay in Deanna's unaffected gaiety and often her wide-eyed innocence. Even when her look was warm and inviting in the stirrings of love she never lost her wistful demureness. There is no real beauty in a face which fails to convey an assurance that a tender heart beats beneath the visible shell. The warmth of Deanna's personality, her charm, her vivacity, and withal an innate sympathy and ready compassion, was reflected in her eyes and on her lips. It was in her spontaneous expression of the best of human qualities that Deanna was truly beautiful. In conjunction with her singing this accounted for the universality of her appeal. And if such an assertion sounds like a panegyric for a very lovely lady, it is none the less appropriate.

All this simply leads me to reflect that in all her screen appearances Deanna exemplified a wonderful femininity which naturally enriched the characters she played, becoming progressively more apparent as the starlet developed into the accomplished star. It seemed to me that in the corporate emotions, the philosophy of these imaginary figures projected on the screen, was embodied much of Deanna's true self, transcending the dictates and objectives of the film-maker and of this I have more to say in a later passage of this book. The ingenue of Deanna's earlier films developed into a young woman of charm, poise and shrewdness, but her unassuming ways were never lost or submerged beneath the new and enticing image. She still retained an engaging candour and vitality and seldom wore a jaded look. That sparkling femininity of hers was never tarnished by experience. In the film 'For The Love Of Mary', when the Hollywood film circuit was about to lose her for always, it was as pervasive as ever when she sang 'I'm cheerful, ever cheerful'. But for me it was always the real Deanna I was watching – not the ambience of herself in make-believe – not Penny, or Connie, or Patricia – nor the demure Anne of 'His Butler's Sister'. They were simply the true goddess, incognito.

Chapter 24

The Film Legend

There can never be a definitive criticism about Deanna Durbin whose career spanned the years of a war of long ago and who left us a legacy of beautiful songs on film and record. And it is to be hoped that in these days of the late twentieth century, on the threshold of a new millennium, electronic wizardry and technical achievement will provide a means of preserving the Deanna Durbin movies, perhaps on some undiscovered material, for posterity, even perhaps enhance their quality. That voice must never be allowed to die or wither on tape or film since, as much as the refinements of intellect or the creativity of genius, it is one of the unexplainable wonders of this world as it might be of any other. For in its splendid octaves lies not only a rare sorcery to enchant the ear, the sweetest therapy for the troubled mind, but a spirituality to warm the living soul.

As I move towards the close of a rather rambling script about a most endearing personality, it seems to me that there might still be aspects of her work during her years of film-making which I have overlooked, that I might have referred to only obliquely, failed wholly to criticise or, having done so, felt that such criticism was less than constructive. So must I in my closing passages strive to atone for any shortcomings in my script and summarise comprehensively what the name Deanna Durbin signifies for me.

The world of entertainment is a grand theatre of illusion and my view, which I am sure others share, is that during her all too brief career Deanna Durbin was in the foremost vanguard of an exclusive company which brought gaiety and gladness into life through one medium or another. And in all her films save 'Christmas Holiday' with its predominant atmosphere of tragedy and moody introspection, a story in which she was completely transformed from the meek Abigail to the gloomy and embittered Jackie, Deanna, under the shrewd and enlightened stewardship of gifted film directors, seemed willingly to subscribe to this formula for generating happiness. She acquired a far-flung host of cinemagoers who loved her for her charming nature as much as her lyric singing in the films in which she starred. Her acting, reinforced by the wondrous pulsations of her marvellous voice, came like a gospel of joy to a cosmopolitan public hungering for a new religion to dispel its fear of war and the imminent threat of war as pagan forces gathered like a dark cloud on every horizon.

Dictators in the West and an aggressor in the Far East were strutting in the international arena, boastful and menacing, sounding the trumpet of doom and of lasting misery which presaged an end to the rule of law among the human race and a democratic and peaceful way of life. Even the despair born of economic depression was something to be regarded as merely an inconvenience in the shadow of a monstrous threat to the morality and stability of civilised life.

The coming of Deanna Durbin to the cinema screen in the late Thirties did much to brighten the hours of leisure for millions. Though only a palliative for woe in the warm seclusion of the cinema, when audiences dispersed they took with them a memory of Summer, of laughter and tears that were solely tears of happiness, of youth and the fond fancies of youth, and perhaps subconsciously the renewal of hope in the face of a very uncertain future. When Deanna's voice rang forth more clearly and sweetly than ever sang the nightingale, how could the heart fail to bound for sheer joy? How could the mind falter in its allegiance to the vision of a world soon to be purged of evil? That vision was idealised in the felicity of Deanna's song. A lovely songstress in her teens was a symbol of all the children of Christendom whose future happiness was at stake, a precious talisman that was never to be despoiled. So in Deanna assuredly a vast host of servicemen in or outside its homelands pictured its own loved ones, both cheering it and reminding it of what the free world was struggling to preserve in an embattled age – not least freedom itself and cherished institutions built up over centuries, above all the continuity and integrity of family life. Nor was it merely a superficial projection of such ideals when two patrolling G.I.s in the film 'Hers To Hold' watched Deanna and her partner make their way from a prohibited beach and agreed in their own simple way that what they had seen of a tender liaison was the perfect example of the sort of thing they were fighting for. I should add that Deanna's part in this symbolism was purely involuntary. For in all her films Deanna was always an individual, invariably lively but subject to dreamy moments of quiet fancy and blissful serenity. Within that circumscription she was never a vehicle for the propagation of ideas or ideology, good or bad, of whatever genesis. Idealism, as far as she was concerned lay in the brilliant characterisation with which she invested the parts she played, especially in 'Christmas Holiday'; perhaps too in some measurable degree in the effusions of a voice which was almost mesmeric in its sweet vibrations. And by way of specific example, in none of her films save 'Lady On A Train' and 'Christmas Holiday' did the concept of evil obtrude itself in a distinctly malevolent way. The psychopaths who sought to dispose of her in these two films were dismal and sullen characters far removed from the wholesome image of the young actors who played opposite Deanna in the thirteen films she made before 'Christmas Holiday'.

Mine may be an old-fashioned attitude, but I maintain that Deanna's whole personality and her remarkable voice are together a medium which can only be correlated with stories of love and romance, innocent and unpretentious, and evolving against dreamy backgrounds either natural or under the gilded roof. And if she was guilty sometimes of roguishness, it did but add to her sparkle.

The very nature of the impressions she kindled in others, of gentleness and tenderness, of selflessness and an instinctive compassion and consideration for others, might well support the conviction that her real talent would have been wasted in repetitive gloomy and turgid melodrama. I would offer this reservation, however, that she acquitted herself more than admirably in 'Christmas Holiday', in which she played the wife of a dissolute gambler, as well as in 'Lady On A Train' in the role of amateur sleuth. Nevertheless, remembering the deep pleasure that was mine watching 'First Love' and 'It Started With Eve' I must confess that I did not enjoy such feeling in respect of the two films in which she had to mix with a lot of unsavoury characters and go in mortal danger of a violent end. Such is my personal preference and I see nothing wrong with the tried formulas in which Deanna excelled. When the unravellings of a plot precluded an interlude or two of music and song, the bright and shining star which was the real Deanna lost some of its lustre.

In the glorious days of her film career Deanna's sweet self and her inimitable voice complimented each other in a perfect way, and thankfully they were recognised by a producer like Pasternak and a director like Henry Koster with whom she made her most enjoyable films. Psychological dramas of death and tragedy were scarcely suitable vehicles for her talents which were orientated towards the bright and cheerful aspects of life, the buoyant spirit, the vivacious mood, the 'living happily ever after' syndrome, if you like. When ordinary folk, humble or not so humble, but all subject to the same tribulations of a fallible society, marched off to the cinema to view the latest Durbin film during the war years they did not go to be traumatised by gloomy Gothic imagery or humourless fantasies about moral decadence and unabated suffering. There was already enough misery in the living world in which they were implanted. What they sought was a brief excursion into the world of fun and laughter, of gaiety and rejoicing, of sunshine and showers which sprinkled but did not drench – a world full of dreams for young and old in which blissful entertainment was preferred to homily and pleasure was the substantive theme – in other words, the world of Deanna Durbin. For her name signified everything that was as beautiful as it was disarming, and withal the indivisible charm of pure melody ranging from the lullaby to the choral hymn, from simple tuneful song to grand aria. Deanna it was who from time to time through the magic of the cinema screen was a radiant visitation in wartime Britain, bringing the elixir of happiness into life which was unquestionably dreary. Her bewitching smile, her merry laughter and the sound of her voice enshrining the inmost soul of music and melody, was like an occasional shaft of light from the New World to the frontiers of the Old. In those dark days Deanna was something of a benediction that all, given kindly fortune, could share. She brought with her the trappings of an idyll to a featureless landscape – a needful escapism for those bowed beneath the grim realities in which (thank God only temporarily) they were immured.

Remembering those days and the pleasure derived from a succession of enchanting films, it was with utter dismay most probably shared by millions that I heard of Deanna's sudden departure from Hollywood and the abandonment of her screen career.

What an incalculable loss that was in the field of entertainment, in particular, musical comedy in which Deanna was unquestionably empress. It is not for me or anyone to speculate on the reasons for such renunciation, only to regret the circumstances which made it necessary or unavoidable. We must be thankful for what is preserved of her remarkable reign.

One point I can make with certainty is that Deanna Durbin will never grow old in the minds of those who remember her as she was in decades which have vanished into the misty corridors of yesteryear. She will always remain young and fair with an unmistakable *joie de vivre* in her blue eyes. That shapely, oval face of hers, ever expressive of a tranquil innocence, will be a recurring vision from the past; which reminds me that a conspicuous feature about all her films, or nearly all, was the complete absence of eroticism. When she played the role of a young woman awakening to love, the effect was spiritual with scarcely a hint of sensuality. When she was in flirtatious mood as in 'Something In The Wind' singing 'You wanna keep your baby lookin' right, dontcher, daddy' there was no suggestion of amorous or sexual intrigue. She was just an adorable being indulging in pure, unadulterated fun. Although she often looked ravishing, it was never her role to parade the blandishments of the courtesan. By the same token I do not believe the young Deanna I saw years ago would have been comfortable in the avant-garde world of today.

Deanna's film career spanned what I would call the Age of Innocence. It was a time when parental supervision in respect of growing children associating with members of the opposite sex was not markedly evident in family behaviour. In those decades before and after the war of 1939-45 sex was something you enjoyed after the wedding. It was not a pre-marital *hors d'oeuvre*. The moral attitude was such that parents took it for granted that their daughters anyway, though aware of shall we say the biological function, would regard their virtue as sacrosanct until they were legally joined in wedlock. Youngsters even in the poorest plebeian circles exercised restraint more through commonsense and intuition than precept. The example of parents as regards sex which had been the fashion for generations was accepted implicitly as the pre-requisite for a happy marriage and a stable family life. On the other hand, the so-called progressive era in which we live today is scornful of the old-time values. The main reason for this is the sordid commercialisation rampant in almost every branch of human activity. The Age of Innocence began to wilt altogether with the swinging Sixties when trendy reformists preached the gospel of 'free love' and encouraged the abandonment of the constraints and the disciplines which had hitherto served as the bedrock of a cohesive and responsible society. The worst iconoclasts perhaps were the unctuous pseudo-psychologists, agony aunts (of both sexes) and do-gooders who, driven by what I can only describe as a false evangelism, used every means of modern communication, the written word as well as radio and television, to inculcate the masses, in particular the young and immature, with their crackpot and insidiously wicked ideas about morality and sexuality, even linking them in a quite presumptuous way with economic ills. They talked of deprivation instead of poverty, of the evils of capitalism instead of the fruits of enterprise or honest toil, of rights instead of responsibilities. To them even heterosexuality was an opprobrious word. What is worse, they affected never to be shocked by deviant behaviour, finding excuse for the most outrageous of human sins. They preached moderation while condoning excess. They were like grand vivisectors of the refined image of mortal man – the heralds and trumpeters of a new Dark Age in which rationality and reason, the bulwarks of civilised life and its corporate endeavour must yield to the spurious idolatry of the 'free spirit', acknowledging no barrier between right and wrong. And so in the Nineties with the battle against moral corruption being waged ever more fiercely, the innocence which may be ascribed to the age in which Deanna grew up and of which she was the personification is under dire threat where still it lingers or is zealously guarded.

Well we might cry 'Alas!' that the sort of films in which Deanna starred and which were so refreshing in her own youth would not be made in the present era by a film industry mainly preoccupied with crime and drugs and sex. The exploitation of the last factor is perhaps the dominant compulsion. A crude deification of the erotic seems to be the primary concern of the mandarins in the entertainment industry. It is they who have changed public taste over the years, who have condoned any form of exhibitionism and loose morality. In a materialistic age it is they first and foremost, since their ideas and productions receive maximum publicity, whose verdict seems to be that civilised proprieties and refined taste are 'old hat'. Television in particular, offering a private cinema screen to every individual, has lowered standards of performance, blatantly so in the musical sphere. The accent on commercialism – the imperative to achieve 'good ratings' as the terminology of today would have it tends to induce the moguls of the film world and their producers not to be too fussy or squeamish about their production or the artists they enlist. They are ever ready to plead that they are simply satisfying public demand, choosing to forget that public taste today is far from being the correct yardstick by which to measure the quality of performance. For that is debased in the sense that it is too complacent about mediocrity. It accepts insults and tasteless jokes as representative of humour – sex, swearing and violence and appallingly bad habits as illustrative of normal family life. The most contemptible piffle doesn't raise a blink, much less a murmur of protest. And the barons of the entertainment world will go on serving up a spate of inferior offerings until perhaps a new reformist spirit generates revulsion against the trash to which an entire generation has become accustomed. The debasement of culture lies at the roots of the current malaise in which brashness and aggression has replaced courtesy and civilised esteem.

What is shown and heard in cinema and theatre today and by implication the television and video screen, is too often degenerate and abysmally puerile. And that means unutterable boredom for people like myself whose memories hark back to their youth in a world where television, to quote one example, had not begun to spread its insidious poison.

When I think of Deanna Durbin singing an 'Old Refrain' as she did in 'The Amazing Mrs Holliday' to a circle of quiet but responsive orphan children lulled by a soul-stirring melody, I find myself wishing that the children and teenagers of the present time could have been raised in a way which would enable them to appreciate the gentler aspects of life, which might have inspired them with feelings of tenderness if they too had witnessed the scene I have described and heard Deanna sing. Alas, I fear their response would be raucous, perhaps even vulgarly contemptuous, solely because they have no clear understanding of the many dimensions of beauty, the parameters of what is good and essential in life. The tendency to jeer and ridicule what is noble and edifying is usually the instinctive reaction of the urban yobs who seem so numerous today. I am almost tempted to include in that category the arrogant and self-appointed innovators in the field of entertainment and especially musical expression and production. In that area their overwhelming preference for pop and disco type of sound displays contempt for those who hunger for 'pure singing', trained voices that are melodious, that are never shrill and are superb in delivery and timing as they used to be in the age when music was disciplined in tempo. If it is possible to approach sublimity in the art of pure singing one need do no more than listen to the performances of Deanna Durbin in her splendid films. These are a legacy which people unborn will come to appreciate as deeply as those who succumbed long ago to the intoxication of her song and over the intervening years have found continual refreshment in viewing those precious films. And what a treasure-house of melody they enfold. One can never tire of vocal marvels like 'La Capinera' from 'Three Smart Girls Grow Up', sung so vivaciously, Tosti's 'Goodbye' from 'Because of Him' and the unforgettable 'Nessun Dorma' from Turandot in 'His Butler's Sister'. In the same mainstream of musical rapture are Mozart's 'Alleluia', 'One Fine Day, Musetta's Waltz Song, Blue Danube Dream, Clavelitos, Vissi D'Arte and that hitherto exclusive male monopoly, 'Largo Al Factotum' from Deanna's first film. Such a list could easily be expanded to include songs which acquired immense popularity all over the world, which, thanks to Deanna, have become familiar to generations past and present. She sang those songs with glorious fervour, a perfect rendition not to be qualified in any respect for the simple reason that perfection is not measured by degrees. And I can only think despairingly of what she might have sung for the world, for her contemporaries as well as posterity, given the propitious circumstances which never did transpire.

Perhaps in this little book which gave me unbounded pleasure to write I have offered a more elaborate assessment of an adorable girl than I intended, and enthused about her exceptional talents, but I cannot think the picture I have presented is overdrawn. Let those who will, accuse me of exaggeration. I would take a very contrary view and insist that what I have written is nothing more or less than a simplification of a genuine belief, namely that Deanna exercised a power of physical attraction and self-expression, supremely articulate in her thrilling voice, which penetrated to the very core of the human spirit. That image to so many of us who could only laud her from afar was something that kindled the most tender affection in our hearts. It made us dream, even to tremble, with delight on innumerable occasions and more than satisfied our romantic sensibilities. Her performance as an actress was distinguished by its candour as much as its charm, a wholly natural charm – and who could resist her roguish affectation when she was in teasing mood? Bashful the one moment, fired with passion the next, capricious, resolute, gentle, spirited, hopeful, despairing, purveying the whole complexity of human emotions with the delicacy and sureness of touch of an accomplished artist, and not least of all a voice of amazing range and sweetness of tone – could any critic be niggardly in the use of superlatives to describe such a combination of talent, versatility and virtue?

You might think that at this point in my survey of the Deanna Durbin Fairy Tale that I have exhausted all possible reference to her qualities and accomplishment. Not so. Apart from being a fine actress and a gifted vocalist of the rarest kind imaginable, she must have been from her earliest youth a more than competent pianist. She was often at the keyboard in her films, notably in 'It Started With Eve' when she gave an energetic rendering of 'When I Sing' for the benefit of a sick man, followed later by 'Clavelitos', and in a later production 'His Butler's Sister' when she sang and played the lovely melody 'When You're Away'. Nor could anyone fault her playing and singing 'Love At Last' in 'Nice Girl?', always aware, be it said, of that distracting pyjama outfit she was wearing.

Deanna also gave the distinct impression in her films of being a talented ballroom dancer. How graceful was her dancing in 'First Love' as Cinderella at the ball! How she whisked round a vast hall in a rippling waltz as she also did in the final scene of 'I'll Be Yours' to the beautiful strains of the Sari Waltz and again to the tune of 'Waltzing In The Clouds' in 'Spring Parade' when her co-star was Robert Cummings. Incidentally, in that old-world romp in a Ruritanian setting Deanna took part in a wild dance with Mischa Auer which must have demanded all her energy as well as her concentration. Nor, by way of complete contrast, must I forget her conga in 'It Started With Eve' with Charles Laughton as her unlikely partner. The tight-fitting evening gown she wore on that occasion showed her trim figure to perfection. Remember her rippling curves and the delightful tossing of her head as she instructed Jonathan Reynolds in the mechanics of the dance – 'One, two, three – kick!', first to the left, then to the right? And how absurd but enjoyable were the gymnastics of her remarkable partner who gave a supreme exhibition as the master of the comic situation which he undoubtedly was. Personally I regretted the premature arrival of Jonathan's son to interrupt the enjoyment of a splendid couple. And I had no time whatever for a loveable tycoon's distracted doctor who was also on hand to spoil his patient's fun.

To linger with 'It Started With Eve' for a moment or two, what a change of atmosphere followed the arrival of two unwelcome newcomers at the night-club! With protestations and baseless accusations levelled at Deanna of betrayal of a promise and a complete lack of principle to serve her ends, it was no wonder that the mood turned to sourness and recrimination. And it was surely just that a grossly insulted young woman should fling a 'Jonathan Special' in her accuser's face. Like so many others, I'll wager, equally absorbed in the action, I thoroughly enjoyed the recipient's discomfiture since he behaved like an ignorant and humourless boor totally lacking in the sensitivity which is a sign of good breeding and calls for good manners at all times in trying situations.

I quote this incident at some length because the sudden transition from delirious fun to dramatic confrontation was an excellent example of the way riotous comedy and serious emotion were blended in Deanna's films, a characteristic which made a decided contribution to their enduring quality. Deanna for her part was usually more sentimental than boisterous, yet on those occasions when she exploded with indignation or righteous anger, one was always inclined to sympathise with her and to feel that such flashes of temperament were wholly justified. Besides, any tantrum was forgivable in one as adorable as Deanna. Her face was ever lit by that inward glow which was so enchanting. I do not speak of magnetism – that is a dubious attribute. But when Deanna smiled she warmed your heart. She was never really capricious; when she was teasing she was tender. When she laughed the impulse was to join in her merriment and savour her delight with a sense of privilege. Perhaps a hint of another emotion too – the reverence which one feels looking upon some precious talisman. Always with this gifted handmaiden of Euterpe was the contradiction of naiveté and the sweet touch of feminine witchery, moreover a disarming beauty bespeaking idealism more than sensuality, to hold one captive beneath its spell.

Chapter 25

Final Reflections

So must I come to the final phase of what has seemed to me to be an excursion into Fairyland.

I never like to forego an opportunity of discussing with those who have the same sympathies as myself the career and the personality of Deanna Durbin. It is a subject of which I could not possibly tire as new reflections occur about her intellectual and spiritual temper, or ideas already thoroughly explored recur, to be burnished perhaps by fresh inspiration and so expand any speculation. It is like having a priceless painting which one examines from all angles through the years to discover new perspectives in one's field of vision, some to become more sharply defined or nebulous according to the variation of light, but all suggesting subtle gradations of colour to stimulate new interest. Simply to say that a fairy-tale figure like the young Deanna Durbin was physically attractive and very talented would be the sort of superficiality giving no real insight into the living being and her motivation. And fundamentally that is why throughout this book I have tried consistently to present a comprehensive and imaginative assessment of a very special and remarkably gifted artist.

It has been said, and it is an opinion voiced by actors themselves, not necessarily only players of some distinction, that the fictitious character of stage and screen gives no guide whatever to the true self, the one who plays the part. My retort to this challenging or controversial remark is that it may very well pass as a broad generalisation, but I maintain that there must be specific instances of dramatisation where the actor or actress invests his or her characterisation with a brilliance which must be derived in a measurable degree from compatibility of personality or spirit. The image as it were becomes a true reflection of the original – the one is an exemplar of the other. Of course, in this connection it might be argued that experience and understanding of human nature applied to the interpretation of stage or screen roles can only add to the plausibility and realism of the performance. And there have been countless masterly exponents of the dramatic art since Man first conceived the fantasy of make-believe both as a source of pleasure and a counter to the hard realities which chafe his mortal life. And it is also very probable that such exponents see in the characters they play more than a passing likeness to their own inner selves, their own peculiarities or whims. They can act therefore with a conviction which accentuates the quality of their performance. Is it not reasonable then, if not axiomatic, to postulate that compatibility between the actor and the image, the reality and the illusion, is likely to be especially true in respect of the younger recruit to the acting profession, one still inexperienced and unspoiled who is unlikely to be prone to worldly or ignoble thoughts and the cynicism which comes of disillusionment and the corruption of ideals. How very true of a young Deanna I hold this to be.

Inasmuch therefore as her films reflected much of her true nature when emotional portrayal was called for, reactions generated by joy or tribulation, and irrespective of the vagaries of the plot, they can be said to give a fair indication of the heart and mind of the principal character herself. That is not so much a generalisation as a premise for conclusions one feels instinctively to be true.

That there were many involved in Deanna's film career from its formative stage until she became a shining star, who sensed a certain exclusivity about their protégé, Koster and Pasternak for instance, is undeniable. It cannot be simply coincidental that the films in which she starred were never in any respect sullied by bad taste. There was never any melodramatic drama or hint of paranoia nor the prolongation of suspense and unbearable tensions culminating in violence – no sensationalism, sex or sordid intrigue. They were never lacquered with the obscenities which are accepted today in the name of realism. Nor were her films of the tedious kind in which unctuous moralists bludgeon an audience with pretentious dialogue. On the contrary, save one exception, they were all engaging comedies, some prolific of pure romanticism ably conceived by script writers and translated beautifully to the cinema screen. I would call them stylish comedies too and their casts were usually amiable, many of them skilled practitioners in a demanding profession. Above all, Deanna's films were ideal in every way for family viewing. They have been referred to by some critics in the past as unsophisticated. I would describe them myself as having the sophistication which is the secret or the flair for true comedy, a culture in itself, situations ingeniously contrived in which humour and wit function in close partnership – where nothing is subjected to derision and where the intrusion of vulgarity or ludicrous slapstick would be unthinkable.

As is often the case with films where there is a perceptible aesthetic structure behind the facade of comedy, humour was often leavened with sentimentality. That is not to suggest that Deanna's films so to speak were embalmed in the emotions that make one weep copiously and inconsolably. There was always the glimmer of a smile to salve semblance of despair or grief, a sense of uninhibited fun waiting to manifest itself once more. Wise indeed were the producers of her era who showed more than a casual regard for the expectations of their audiences or indeed their preference, especially the vast majority who had no wish to be dowsed in misery and who sought the kind of escapism in which Deanna, as a gifted purveyor, can truly be said to have excelled. A notable characteristic too of Deanna's films was that their continuity was invariably clear and unbroken, the characterisation more than admirable and the action, though free of violence, always stimulating, if sometimes with a touch of absurdity about it, but ever disarming and conducive to laughter. I venture to suggest that the stories were chosen selectively for Deanna to demonstrate her engaging talents, foremost of all the rippling octaves of her marvellous voice. Nor were they ever perfunctory in execution unlike many scripts today where the concept of drama seems to be sustained dialogue in drawing-room or bedroom, and protagonists, often lacking in culture or mutual sympathy, who have little of consequence to offer and whose main characteristic is a flexile tongue. Nothing is more boring than a film in which the studio is the main venue for the inane clacking of uninspired performers who sound as weary of their roles as a cinema audience finds it impossible to become engrossed in what purports to be a vehicle for their pleasure.

Knowing so much of the precise detail of Deanna's films from the good fortune of having viewed them so often, I find myself in pensive moments recreating in my mind so many scenes from those romantic musicals. I can so easily recall the inflexions of a familiar voice and the occasions in question, the changes in her expression, the immense range of her musical rendition. I can close my eyes and envision that lake in 'I'll Be Yours', save that I am the occupant of the boat which glides dreamily across placid waters. I enter as it were a palace of dreams and she is the chatelaine who unlocks the door and holds court in grand and magical estate. Had Deanna been born in an older, mythological time she would have been a princess in Parnassus and created another golden legend for posterity.

The fact that Deanna came from obscurity in a sudden blaze of publicity, flashed like a comet across the cinema screen for a few brief years and then vanished as suddenly as she came invests her almost with an air of mystery. It is easy to use the word 'legendary' in respect of one who, so swiftly acclaimed as a mistress of her art, won the admiration and love of millions scattered across a terrestrial globe which had never seen her like before. The reasons for her sudden disappearance from the cinema screen are of less importance and much less relevant than the fact that she brightened the lives of so many during the years when the very hint of a new Durbin film on the way was something to quicken the pulse and excite the imagination of those familiar with her talents and her unfailing charm. Hers was a fortunate and happy interlude in the history of the cinema, though I fear she has never been given sufficient credit for her delightful impersonations and the wistful imagery she wove of a world where love and romance were conjoined in blissful harmony and every tomorrow was a threshold for joy. Nor has proper tribute been accorded her for her tremendous attraction as a singer – the singular quality of a truly remarkable voice.

In 'It Started With Eve' Charles Laughton, as a rather crotchety, old millionaire, commenting on a young woman whom he believed to be his son's fiancée, remarked 'But she seemed such a nice girl – so mild and gentle,' or some similar phraseology. Verily, there was a mildness and gentility called for in so many of her roles and I am sure she had no difficulty whatsoever in behaving in a soft and yielding way as part of the compassionate and sympathetic traits that were inborn in her. And the point I wish to make here by this reference to her capacity for warm goodwill and tenderness is that it tended to disguise the fact that there was a strong will and extraordinary strength of character beneath her gentle exterior.

As I conclude this celebration of a gifted actress and singer and a most endearing personality, I can only repeat my conviction that there are countless others like myself who will ever be grateful for the hours of joy and extreme pleasure she gave us in abundance during her film career as well as the memories we would cherish thereafter, memories which, thanks to modern technology, can be enlivened in a practical way. And before finally closing this testament let me but say 'God speed', to Deanna Durbin and all she holds dear. I reflect that her fairy tale existence in this world with its gentle symphonies of hope and love and laughter, its immeasurable bliss and its rich tapestry of song, burgeoned in a world overshadowed by war and the threat of war. But her Summer in terms of her screen appearances, her appealing public image, had hardly begun before she was whisked away to another land, ancient and mellow, and a happy private life among family and friends. Yet that is a blessing than which in respect of personal contentment and spiritual fulfilment there is no greater treasure that mortal existence has to offer. Let Winter come therefore as come it must, and all that it portends – the memory of Deanna's voice, the reality of her being, shall be with those of us who basked in the blaze of her Springtime. Such wonders shall never be lost as they drift like all beautiful and ethereal things down the long and immemorial avenues of Time.